Poetry

Novels and short stories

The exams

Homework diary

Topic	Score
Punctuation again!	/35
Punctuation writing	/40
Uses of commas	/35
Punctuating speech	/65
Apostrophes	/35
Types of sentence	/35
Spellings	/15
Words often misspelt	/35
Homophones	/35
Organising ideas	/30
Linking words and phrases	/45
Improving writing style	/35
Speaking and listening 1	/26
Speaking and listening 2	/31
Original writing	/19
Personal writing	/10
Essay writing	/23
The media	/20
Film grammar: sound	/25
Film grammar: camera shots	/30
Film grammar: camera movements	/40
Film grammar: editing	/15
Shakespeare assignment	/5
Shakespeare's imagery	/20
Essay notes on Caliban	/15
Spidergrams	/21
Studying poetry	/28
Writing about poetry	/17
Comparing poems	/25
ELH poems 1	/23
ELH poems 2	/38
Poetry of other cultures 1	/37
Poetry of other cultures 2	/33
Novels and short stories 1	/35
Novels and short stories 2	/19
Literary technique 1	/13
Literary technique 2	/33
Short stories	/34
Exam technique	/31

Exam hints

There are two major ways to revise for English:

- Studying your set texts – This should be active rather than passive. Make notes; don't just read things through.
- Practising key skills – Ideally you should do this under timed conditions so you can cope better in the exam.

Planning

- Find out the dates of your exams and make an examination and revision timetable.
- Make sure you know which texts are required for each exam. If you have revised a text in class, write down the key points from memory and then check them against your notes.
- If you have completed a practice piece, look most carefully at areas that need improving.

Revising

- Revise in short bursts of about 30 minutes, followed by a short break.
- Learn facts from your exercise books, notebooks and Success guide.
- Do the multiple choice and quiz-style questions in this book and check your solutions to see how much you know.
- Once you feel confident that you know the topic, do the examination-style questions in this book. Highlight the key words in the question, plan your answer and then go back and check that you have answered the question.
- Make a note of any topics that you do not understand and go back through the notes again.
- Use the homework diary to keep track of the topics you have covered, and your scores.

Getting ready for the examination

- Read the instructions carefully and do what you are asked to do: if there are five marks you'll probably have to give five details, and so on.
- Pay particular attention to such things as layout and images in the Media text on Paper 1.
- Skim texts first to get a general idea, then scan for details.
- In the reading paper do not get bogged down on one question. You will gain most marks if you attempt all questions.
- Remember to use the Point, Example, Comment rule when commenting on texts.
- Know your texts. That way you won't waste time looking for quotations. Keep quotations short and to the point.
- Last but not least: don't panic! If you've followed the advice above, you'll certainly have done your best.

Good luck!

Punctuation again!

A

For each of the sentences below choose the one that is correctly punctuated.

1 a) The arrow tipped with deadly poison rushed towards me.
b) The arrow, tipped with deadly poison, rushed towards me.
c) The arrow (tipped with deadly poison) rushed towards me
d) The arrow tipped with deadly poison, rushed towards me. **(1 mark)**

2 a) Dont move she shouted!
b) 'Don't move!' she shouted.
c) Don't move, she shouted.
d) 'Don't move,' she shouted. **(1 mark)**

3 a) Simon Armitages poems aren't very difficult to understand.
b) Simon Armitage's poems arent very difficult to understand.
c) Simon Armitage's poems aren't very difficult to understand.
d) Simon Armitages' poems aren't very difficult to understand. **(1 mark)**

4 a) However you looked at it from the wrong point of view.
b) However you looked at it, from the wrong point of view.
c) However, you looked at it, from the wrong point of view.
d) However, you looked at it from the wrong point of view. **(1 mark)**

5 a) 'Where,' asked Emma, 'did you leave your coat?'
b) 'Where?' asked Emma, 'did you leave your coat.'
c) 'Where' asked Emma, 'Did you leave your coat?'
d) 'Where,' asked Emma, 'did you leave you're coat?' **(1 mark)**

Score / 5

B

There are ten punctuation errors in the following paragraph. Circle the errors and write out the correct words.

It was almost ten o clock when I woke up. My alarm clock was connected by radio to some sort of N.A.T.O. supercomputer and was guaranteed accurate to one millionth of a second per century. Unfortunately I forgot to turn it on before I went to sleep. 'Great.' I said to myself as I rushed down the stairs, 'thats just what I need.' Fortunately for me, the buses arent very crowded at that time in the morning and I got to work in less than half an hour.

'Ah, Mr Anderson,' said my boss, 'working flexi-time are we.'

'Sorry,' I murmured, 'I was at the dentists.'

'Well, if youd let us know in advance,' he said as he wandered off.

....

....

....

(10 marks)

Score / 10

C

This is a coursework practice question. Plan your answer here and write your response on separate paper.

Original writing coursework

Write a story suitable for teenagers on one of the following topics:

- The prisoner
- A difficult case
- Lost

You should think about:

- making your story interesting for its intended audience
- how your story is structured
- using appropriate language in the narrative and in any dialogue you include
- using a variety of sentences and paragraphs
- correct spelling
- correct punctuation.

Score / 20

For more on this topic see pages 6–29 of your Success Guide.

Total score / 35

How well did you do? 0–7 Try again 8–18 Getting there 19–27 Good work 28–35 Excellent!

Punctuation writing

A

Choose just one answer, a, b, c or d.

1 Which of the following does not use a semi-colon correctly? (1 mark)

a) Three people slept in the haunted house; none of them returned unscathed.
b) Jared made a list: matches for the fire; a book to read; extra chocolate and a torch.
c) Michaela went for a walk; Ian had a bath.
d) MACBETH. Thou canst not say I did it; never shake thy gory locks at me.

2 Which of the following sentences does not use a colon correctly? (1 mark)

a) I wondered if anybody was there: I went to see.
b) Everyone gathered in the hall: the cook, the butler, the two maids and the footman.
c) Prospero says: 'We are such stuff as dreams are made on.'
d) That day they appointed: a new manager; a new deputy manager and two machinists.

3 Which punctuation mark is commonly replaced by a dash? (1 mark)

a) the colon
b) the semi-colon
c) both colons and semi-colons
d) semi-colons in lists

4 Which punctuation mark is not followed by a capital letter? (1 mark)

a) the colon
b) the semi-colon
c) exclamation marks
d) question marks

5 A rhetorical question does not (1 mark)

a) begin with 'what' or 'where'
b) require a question mark
c) have to be followed by a capital letter
d) require an answer

Score /5

B

The following paragraph is unpunctuated. Rewrite it correctly.

Almost all of the people in charge the captain the first mate the chief petty officer and the other senior members of the crew were surprised when the news came through the ship was sinking if they had been down in the engine room they would have had a very different view of things the surprise was not that the ship was sinking but that it had ever floated in the first place when the captain found me I was knee deep in water is there anything we can do he said I paused for a second or two and then said man the lifeboats (20 marks)

Score /20

C

This is an exam preparation question. Answer all parts of the question on a separate piece of paper.

The purpose of punctuation is to make your writing as clear as possible to the reader. The following sentences are ambiguous. Repunctuate them so that they make sense. Do not alter any of the words.

1. **Because of his unreliability the play was delayed.**
2. **Ferdinand Magellan was the first man to sail round the world he discovered the Straits of Magellan in 1520.**
3. **Frances put the plant on the windowsill so it could get more sun.**
4. **Gemma is a very reliable student, she never misses deadlines.**
5. **Healthy eating is good for you it should not be overdone.**
6. **I did not go on the outing instead I went to see a film.**
7. **I was so tired I had worked solidly for three hours.**

8. **King Charles I walked and talked ten minutes after his head was cut off.**
9. **Please report to the office if you have any of the following notes of absence dinner money.**
10. **Science is a difficult subject many students hate it.**
11. **Stephen, the boy with the black coat took the ball.**
12. **There was only one problem Henry knew the answer.**
13. **After we ate the neighbours came to see us.**
14. **Wherever I go my friend the doctor goes with me.**
15. **Nothing has happened since nothing could happen.**

Score / 15

For more on this topic see pages 6–29 of your Success Guide.

Total score / 40

How well did you do? 0–8 Try again 9–20 Getting there 21–31 Good work 32–40 Excellent!

Uses of commas

A

For each of the sentences below choose the one that is correctly punctuated.

1 a) The 'Mayor of Casterbridge' is one of my favourite novels.
b) The 'Mayor Of Casterbridge' is one of my favourite novels.
c) The 'Mayor of casterbridge' is one of my favourite novels.
d) The 'mayor of casterbridge' is one of my favourite novels. **(1 mark)**

2 a) The B.B.C. did a very good adaptation of Jane Austen's 'Pride and Prejudice' recently.
b) The BBC did a very good adaptation of Jane Austens 'Pride and Prejudice' recently.
c) The BBC did a very good adaptation of Jane Austen's 'Pride and Prejudice' recently.
d) The B.B.C. did a very good adaptation of Jane Austens Pride and Prejudice recently. **(1 mark)**

3 a) Nobody knows where the word dog comes from.
b) Nobody knows where the word 'dog' comes from.
c) Nobody knows where the word <dog> comes from.
d) Nobody knows where the word, dog, comes from. **(1 mark)**

4 a) The line 'Alas! Poor Yorick! I knew him, Horatio.' from Hamlet is often misquoted.
b) The line: Alas! Poor Yorick! I knew him, Horatio; from 'Hamlet' is often misquoted.
c) The line 'Alas! Poor Yorick! I knew him, Horatio.' From 'Hamlet' is often misquoted.
d) The line 'Alas! Poor Yorick! I knew him, Horatio.' from 'Hamlet' is often misquoted. **(1 mark)**

5 a) The first sentence of Dickens's 'Bleak House' is the single word 'November'.
b) The first sentence of Dickens' 'Bleak House' is the single word 'November'.
c) The first sentence of Dickens 'Bleak House' is the single word: November.
d) The first sentence of Dickens' Bleak House is the single word 'November.' **(1 mark)**

Score / 5

B

The following piece of writing has ten errors involving punctuation. Write it out correctly.

The opening line of Tennysons poem the eagle is very striking.
'He clasps the crag with crooked hands'
The most noticeable thing about it is the use of the word hands where the reader might have expected something like talons or claws. The second thing that makes the line striking is the alliteration on the letter c. The repeated cs give the line a harsh sound which is in keeping with the eagles harsh environment.

....

....

....

....

....

Score / 10

C **This is a GCSE-style question. Answer all parts of the question. Continue on separate sheets of paper where necessary.**

Discussing a poem

Write a commentary on the following poem. Remember to use quotations to back up your points and to lay these out correctly.

The Eagle

He clasps the crag with crooked hands;
Close to the sun in lonely lands,
Ring'd with the azure world, he stands.
The wrinkled sea beneath him crawls;
He watches from his mountain walls,
And like a thunderbolt he falls.

Alfred Tennyson

Score / 20

For more on this topic see pages 6–29 of your Success Guide.

Total score / 35

How well did you do? 0–7 Try again 8–18 Getting there 19–27 Good work 28–35 Excellent!

Punctuating speech

A

Choose just one answer, a, b, c or d.

1 Inverted commas are not used to show (1 mark)

a) when someone is being ironic
b) when someone is speaking
c) the actual words someone said
d) when something is upside down

2 Direct speech is (1 mark)

a) when someone addresses you personally
b) separated from the rest of a sentence by a punctuation mark
c) only used in play scripts
d) more forthright than indirect speech

3 Direct speech (1 mark)

a) begins with a capital letter
b) only starts with a capital letter if it is preceded by a full stop
c) carries on the punctuation of the sentence that introduces it
d) is punctuated according to how it is pronounced

4 When writing down direct speech you should always (1 mark)

a) start each thing said on a new line
b) begin a new line for each new speaker
c) indent your paragraphs
d) make it clear who is speaking by using a statement marker

5 Indirect speech is (1 mark)

a) when you say something indirectly
b) punctuated in the same way as direct speech
c) when you report what is said without using the exact words
d) punctuated using single inverted commas

Score /5

B

Below is a conversation that has not been punctuated or laid out properly. Write it out correctly.

What would you like to eat asked Danielle, as she searched through the cupboards. I don't know said Karen what have you got? Well there's pasta, rice and various sauces said Danielle. Do you fancy Italian or Chinese? Chinese I think. OK, then what can we have with it? I think there's some salad in the fridge. That'll be fine.

....

....

....

....

....

....

....

....

Score /25

C This is an exam preparation question. Answer both parts of the question.

Direct and indirect speech

You can add variety to your writing by varying the way in which you convey speech.
In direct speech you write down the actual words spoken.
In indirect speech you report on what was said.

1 Change the following piece of indirect speech into direct speech. **(20 marks)**

My friend Clare had an argument with her dad. She was just going out and he wanted to know what time she'd be back. She said she didn't know so he got annoyed and gave her a grilling about who she was going with, where she was going, whether there'd be any boys or alcohol. Clare just gave vague answers but then she said she hadn't got time for all that and stormed out.

....

....

....

....

....

....

2 Change the following piece of direct speech into reported speech. **(15 marks)**

'Where's the pen I lent you?' said James.
'I thought I gave it back to you,' said Richard.
'That's what you always say!' said James. 'This is the last time I lend you anything.'
'But I did,' protested Richard. 'There it is in your pocket.'
'Oh,' said James.

....

....

....

....

....

Make brief notes here on the advantages and disadvantages of direct and indirect speech.

....

....

....

....

Score /35

For more on this topic see pages 6–29 of your Success Guide.

Total score /65

How well did you do? ✗ 0–13 Try again 14–33 Getting there 34–50 Good work 51–65 Excellent! ✓

Apostrophes

A

Choose just one answer, a, b, c or d.

1 Which of the following is not a possessive pronoun? (1 mark)

a) his
b) it's
c) mine
d) theirs

2 Which of the following possessive plurals is correctly punctuated? (1 mark)

a) the childrens' game
b) the Jone's house
c) the women's team
d) the Charles Dicken's Museum

3 Which of the following apostrophes is incorrect? (1 mark)

a) I'm going out at eight o'clock.
b) Hannas' friend is called Martha.
c) Where'd you leave your coat?
d) The house hasn't been painted in years.

4 Which of the following sentences needs an apostrophe? (1 mark)

a) We travelled in Charles car.
b) The Shakespeares lived in Stratford-on-Avon.
c) I want to go to the Tate Modern.
d) The horses broke into a canter.

5 The boy's bikes indicates that (1 mark)

a) there are several boys with a several bikes
b) there is one boy with several bikes
c) there are several boys with one bike each
d) there are several bikes all belonging to boys

Score / 5

B

The following piece of dialogue has eleven errors involving apostrophes. Write it out correctly.

Nigel Hi! Didnt know you were goin to be here
Keri Yea, well, I changed my mind didnt I?
Nigel Whend you get ere?
Keri Bout eight oclock. Couldve been earlier, dunno.
Nigel Are you and the others going to Nicks party?
Keri Yea, were thinkin about it.

....
....
....
....
....
....
....
....

Score / 10

C This is an exam preparation question.

Writing dialogue

One way of showing your understanding of a text is to carry on a scene from a play or to add an extra scene. Use the space below to add an extra scene to a play that you have studied.

Name of play ______

Characters involved ______

How your scene fits into the play? ______

______

______

Begin your dialogue here. ______

______

______

______

______

______

______

Score / 20

For more on this topic see pages 6–29 of your Success Guide.

Total score / 35

How well did you do? ✗ 0–7 Try again 8–18 Getting there 19–27 Good work 28–35 Excellent! ✓

Types of sentence

A

There are four types of sentence in English: simple, compound, complex and minor. For each of the following identify the sentence type.

1 Alan left this morning. (1 mark)

a) simple
b) compound
c) complex
d) minor

2 Get out! (1 mark)

a) simple
b) compound
c) complex
d) minor

3 Geography and drama are my favourite subjects. (1 mark)

a) simple
b) compound
c) complex
d) minor

4 I didn't go to the match on Saturday, although I wanted to. (1 mark)

a) simple
b) compound
c) complex
d) minor

5 Rebecca bought a new CD and I bought a present for my mum. (1 mark)

a) simple
b) compound
c) complex
d) minor

Score / 5

B

Read the definition of a compound sentence and answer the questions that follow.

Compound sentences are joined by coordinating conjunctions like 'and'. Complex sentences are joined by subordinating conjunctions such as 'because'.

1 In the sentence below, underline the conjunction being used and then label it as either coordinating or subordinating. (5 marks)

a) Two buses arrived but both buses were full. ....
b) They won't let you in the play if you don't arrive on time. ....
c) We lost the match because we didn't have enough experience. ....
d) He could force the door or he could break in through a window. ....
e) We had a really good time until the money ran out. ....

2 In the following paragraph too many compound sentences have been used. Rewrite the paragraph using a variety of sentence types. (You might also wish to change some of the pronouns to proper nouns.) (5 marks)

It was late and it was dark and Hudd decided to call it a day and head for his car. He walked slowly as there was always a possibility of being followed in his line of work and he didn't like the idea of being jumped on in some murky car park a long way from help without even having anything to pick up and hit his assailant with. He thought about the case as he was going along and he didn't like what he was thinking as there were too many clues and too few answers. The car park was virtually deserted apart from his own car and a rather beat-up old van that was sitting in one corner with its engine running but with no obvious driver.

Score / 10

C These are exam preparation questions. Answer both questions. Continue on separate sheets of paper where necessary.

1 Describe a place you know well. Remember to use a variety of sentence types. (10 marks)

....

....

....

....

....

....

....

....

....

2 Write the opening of a detective story. Remember to use a variety of sentence types. (10 marks)

....

....

....

....

....

....

....

Score / 20

For more on this topic see pages 6–29 of your Success Guide.

Total score / 35

How well did you do? 0–7 Try again 8–18 Getting there 19–27 Good work 28–35 Excellent!

Spellings

A

Choose just one answer, a, b, c or d.

1 Which of the following words is from a different word family? (1 mark)

a) machine
b) mechanical
c) machinery
d) papier-mâché

2 Which of the following words is from a different word family? (1 mark)

a) government
b) hangover
c) governor
d) governess

3 Which of the following words is from a different word family? (1 mark)

a) alienation
b) national
c) international
d) nationhood

4 Which of the following words is from a different word family? (1 mark)

a) assumption
b) consumption
c) summary
d) sumptuous

5 Which of the following words is from a different word family? (1 mark)

a) predict
b) dictionary
c) addict
d) dictation

Score /5

B

1 What is a mnemonic? (2 marks)

....

2 Write down a mnemonic you use, or have used, to help you to remember a spelling. (2 marks)

....

3 What is the name for words that have the same sound but different spellings? (2 marks)

....

4 Why do these words not show up when you are using a spell check? (2 marks)

....

5 Write down the irregular plural forms of the following words.
Dwarf, hoof, shelf, knife, life, half (2 marks)

....

Score /10

C This is an exam preparation exercise.

At GCSE all of your exams (except for English) have extra marks available for good spelling, punctuation and grammar. In science you will not gain the extra marks if you misspell scientific words, and so on. English is the only exam in which you lose marks for poor spelling. In the English exam you will be penalised most for misspelling common words.

1 Subject specific words

Do you have problems spelling 'parallel' in Maths, 'onomatopoeia' in English or 'appeasement' in History? In the space below write down the five words that you have most trouble spelling and work out a mnemonic for each one.

Word	....	Mnemonic	....
Word	....	Mnemonic	....
Word	....	Mnemonic	....
Word	....	Mnemonic	....
Word	....	Mnemonic	....

2 Homophones

The commonest spelling errors occur with homophones. In the space below write out a rule for telling each homophone apart.

Homophone	Rule
There, their, they're	....
Your, you're	....
It's, its	....
Where, wear	....
Were, we're	....
Principal, principle	....

3 Irregular spellings – some spelling just have to be learned.
Use the Look, Cover, Write, Check method on the spellings below.

Look	Cover	Write	Check
a) Strength			
b) Straight			
c) February			
d) Library			
e) Subtle			

For more on this topic see pages 6–29 of your Success Guide.

Total score / 15

How well did you do? 0–3 Try again 4–8 Getting there 9–12 Good work 13–15 Excellent!

Words often misspelt

A

Each of the sentences below has two possible spelling errors. Choose the sentence in which both words are spelled correctly.

1 a) We can't decide whether to go to the Mediteranean or the Caribbean for our holidays.
b) We can't decide whether to go to the Mediterranean or the Caribbean for our holidays.
c) We can't decide whether to go to the Mediteranean or the Carribean for our holidays.
d) We can't decide whether to go to the Mediteranean or the Caribean for our holidays. **(1 mark)**

2 a) We wouldn't recommend accommodation at that hotel.
b) We wouldn't recomend acommodation at that hotel.
c) We wouldn't recommend acommodation at that hotel.
d) We wouldn't recomend accommodation at that hotel. **(1 mark)**

3 a) I wish the Principle would practise what he preaches.
b) I wish the Principle would practice what he preaches.
c) I wish the Principal would practice what he preaches.
d) I wish the Principal would practise what he preaches **(1 mark)**

4 a) Waiting was unecessary becuse of the good organisation.
b) Waiting was unnecesary beccause of the good organisation.
c) Waiting was unneccessary because of the good organisation.
d) Waiting was unnecessary because of the good organisation. **(1 mark)**

5 a) The weather was definately beginning to improve.
b) The weather was definitely begining to improve.
c) The weather was definitely beginning to improve.
d) The weather was definately begining to improve. **(1 mark)**

Score / 5

B

The following piece of writing has ten spelling errors. Write it out correctly in the space below.

I started working in advertising because I wanted a job that was glamourous. I thought that I'd be meeting beutiful models and famous photographers. The onely model I have met so far is a model of the Eiffel Tower that we used in an advertisment for some French dressing. Its not bad work, writting advertising copy all day, but is definately not as exsiting as I thought it was going to be. I sometimes get inpatient with my boss but nobodies perfect.

....

....

....

....

....

Score / 10

C This is a GCSE-style question.

Write an article for a school magazine in which you explain some of the problems you have had with spelling and how you overcame them.

You should:

- write in a friendly and informal style
- aim for a light tone
- offer some tips that might help others.

Score / 20

For more on this topic see pages 6–29 of your Success Guide.

Total score / 35

How well did you do? ✗ 0–7 Try again 8–18 Getting there 19–27 Good work 28–35 Excellent! ✓

Homophones

A

For each of the sentences below choose the one that is spelled correctly.

1 a) They got into there car and drove away.
b) They got into they're car and drove away.
c) They got into their car and drove away.
d) They got into thier car and drove away. **(1 mark)**

2 a) You're late.
b) Your late.
c) Your' late.
d) Youre late. **(1 mark)**

3 a) Where did you buy your rainware?
b) Wear did you buy your rainware?
c) We're did you buy your rainwear?
d) Where did you buy your rainwear? **(1 mark)**

4 a) I didn't here that you were here until yesterday.
b) I didn't hear that you were here until yesterday.
c) I didn't here that you were here until yesterday.
d) I didn't hear that you were hear until yesterday. **(1 mark)**

5 a) It's the first time I've seen the dog leave it's dinner.
b) Its the first time I've seen the dog leave it's dinner.
c) It's the first time I've seen the dog leave its dinner.
d) Its the first time I've seen the dog leave its dinner. **(1 mark)**

Score / 5

B

The following piece of writing has ten spelling errors. Write it out correctly.

The new software is called 'ANYWARE'. It's a solution for the problem of mobile computer users who don't know wear they will be working from day to day. If you have ANYWARE installed it doesn't matter were you are; the software detects the local network node and does it's stuff. It works out where you are as long as youre computer is 'Bluetooth' compatible and your not to far from a node. In theory you could be driving in a car through a city and the software would keep you're network connection running by jumping from node to node. Another use might be in computers sewn into you're clothing. The network would know were you were at all times and could reroute all your electronic data to the jacket your wearing. We're thinking of calling that version of the software 'ANYWEAR'.

....

....

....

....

....

....

....

Score / 10

C

This is a GCSE-style question.

Write a set of instructions for a common task such as making a pot of tea or tying a pair of shoelaces.
You should write in a friendly and informal style, addressing your reader as 'you'.

Score / 20

For more on this topic see pages 6–29 of your Success Guide.

Total score / 35

How well did you do? ✗ 0–7 Try again 8–18 Getting there 19–27 Good work 28–35 Excellent! ✓

Organising ideas

A

Choose just one answer, a, b, c or d.

1 A paragraph should contain (1 mark)

a) at least three sentences
b) a main idea
c) a mixture of ideas
d) a concluding sentence

2 Well organised paragraphs contain (1 mark)

a) ideas linked by connectives
b) examples and illustrations
c) a topic sentence
d) all of the above

3 Topic sentences usually occur (1 mark)

a) at the end
b) anywhere that is appropriate
c) in the middle
d) at the beginning

4 Which of the following is not a sequencing connective? (1 mark)

a) and
b) eventually
c) unless
d) subsequently

5 Some linking and sequencing phrases can be overused. Which of the following is a cliché? (1 mark)

a) at the end of the day
b) when all's said and done
c) when it comes down to it
d) all of the above

Score /5

B

Here are some notes for a paragraph on the birth of a star.
Rewrite them using linking and sequencing words.

Massive cloud of hydrogen – gravity pulls it together – hydrogen at centre gets crushed – nuclear reaction takes place – two hydrogen atoms become one helium atom – great deal of energy released – a star is born.

....
....
....
....
....
....
....
....
....
....
....

Score /5

C **This is an exam preparation question.**

Often topic sentences on their own can give you an idea of the content of a text. (You use this fact when skim-reading.)

Below are the topic sentences for a piece of descriptive writing. Complete the paragraphs.

The old house had been deserted for years.

....

....

....

....

Once I had managed to get the door to open I was able to see into the hallway.

....

....

....

When I progressed into the living room I began to worry that the flooring might not be safe.

....

....

....

After some hesitation I decided not to attempt the stairs and made my way into what must have been the library.

....

....

....

I was astonished by what I read in the tattered old journal.

....

....

....

I was just about to leave when a shelf full of novels by Dickens caught my eye; they were all arranged in alphabetical order of title except one.

....

....

....

.... So, this was the answer to the mystery.

Score / 20

For more on this topic see pages 6–29 of your Success Guide. Total score / 30

How well did you do? 0–6 Try again 7–15 Getting there 16–23 Good work 24–30 Excellent!

Linking words and phrases

A

Choose just one answer, a, b, c or d.

1 **Which of the following words is not a linking connective?** (1 mark)

a) firstly
b) furthermore
c) in addition
d) moreover

2 **Which of the following words or phrases can be used to show an opinion?** (1 mark)

a) above all
b) it would seem
c) for example
d) furthermore

3 **Which word below is best suited for ordering a piece of writing?** (1 mark)

a) except
b) naturally
c) therefore
d) firstly

4 **Which of the following words or phrases can be used to compare?** (1 mark)

a) in contrast
b) subsequently
c) similarly
d) significantly

5 **Which of the following words works best in a conclusion?** (1 mark)

a) nevertheless
b) throughout
c) notwithstanding
d) furthermore

Score / 5

B

The following paragraph is poorly sequenced. Write a better organised account.

Making a cup of tea isn't all that difficult. You pour the tea from the pot into a cup and add milk. Some people like to warm the pot before adding the hot water and some people like to put the milk in the cup first. Then you add sugar if you like it. Obviously you need to have all these things ready beforehand.

....

....

....

....

....

Score / 10

C **This is a GCSE-style question. Answer all parts of the question. Continue on separate sheets of paper where necessary.**

Write a description of a job you have undertaken. This could be a single project or your regular part-time occupation. Include the following sections:

what you did – use sequencing words here
how you did it – provide examples here
whether you were successful – express your opinions in this section
what you learned – this will be your conclusion

What I did

....

....

....

....

....

How I did it

....

....

....

....

....

Whether I was successful

....

....

....

....

....

What I learned

....

....

....

....

....

Score / 30

For more on this topic see pages 6–29 of your Success Guide.

Total score / 45

How well did you do? ✗ 0–9 Try again 10–23 Getting there 24–35 Good work 36–45 Excellent! ✓

Improving writing style

A

Choose just one answer, a, b, c or d.

1 Short sentences can be used (1 mark)

a) to build tension
b) to show that you have control of sentence punctuation
c) to move the story on quickly
d) to start a story slowly

2 Which of the following is not a cliché? (1 mark)

a) Clichés should be avoided like the plague.
b) The use of clichés leaves much to be desired.
c) A cliché is a phrase that is no longer outré.
d) You should leave no stone unturned in eliminating clichés.

3 Brevity is (1 mark)

a) a goal much to be desired
b) one of the key elements in a mature style
c) apposite on almost any occasion
d) good

4 Which of the following is not an example of tautology? (1 mark)

a) puzzling mystery
b) unnecessary and redundant
c) dead and buried
d) ultimate conclusion

5 In a stylish, effective sentence the most important part is (1 mark)

a) at the start
b) at the end
c) in the middle
d) where it fits best

Score /5

B

Rewrite the following paragraph to give it more tension.

The coach made its way up the hill and the day darkened around it until complete and total night had fallen. The coachman was nervous as he knew that this road was hazardous and dangerous. Only last week a coach had disappeared into thin air. Suddenly, without warning the horses reared and bucked, the creaky old coach gave up the ghost and ground to a halt. The coachman reached for the pistol he always carried with him in case of emergencies and shouted 'Who's there' into the darkness that now blanketed the land, but there was no reply or response.

....

....

....

....

....

....

....

Score /10

C

This is an exam preparation question.

Original writing

Practise improving your style. Write the opening paragraph of a story entitled 'Why I should have stayed in bed' in the space below. Write as quickly as you can to let your ideas flow. In the second space redraft the paragraph using some of the ideas you have explored about better style.

Version 1

....

....

....

....

....

....

....

....

....

....

....

Version 2

....

....

....

....

....

....

....

....

....

....

....

Now compare the two versions. Give yourself marks up to 20 for each improvement you have made.

Score / 20

For more on this topic see pages 6–29 of your Success Guide.

Total score / 35

How well did you do? 0–7 Try again 8–18 Getting there 19–27 Good work 28–35 Excellent!

Speaking and listening 1

A

Choose just one answer, a, b, c or d.

1 Standard English is used in most talks because (1 mark)

a) it gains you more marks
b) people respond better to Standard English
c) it can be used to address the widest audience
d) it is usually associated with explanations

2 A good talk is almost always (1 mark)

a) about an interesting subject
b) well structured and prepared
c) funny
d) informative

3 Brainstorming is (1 mark)

a) a good method of structuring your talk
b) a good way of planning your talk
c) a good way of discussing a topic
d) a good way of producing ideas for your talk

4 A good way to give a fluent talk is (1 mark)

a) to write it out completely and learn it off by heart
b) to make sure it has a beginning, middle and end
c) to write key phrases on pieces of card as prompts
d) to choose a subject you know really well

5 Which of the following is the most important factor when delivering a successful talk (1 mark)

a) matching the subject of your talk with your audience
b) providing opportunities for audience interaction
c) standing up straight
d) appearing relaxed and confident

Score / 5

B

Below is a transcript of a part of a talk given by a student. Read it carefully and answer the question that follows.

Well ... the ... the Island in Lord of the Flies is a sort of laboratory that William Golding has set up. It's like he said, 'What would really happen if a group of boys was ... were stranded on a desert island. He couldn't find out by putting a group of real boys on a real island so he wrote the novel as a ... thought experiment. He decided on that ... and he let things take their course as any scientist would. Once the boys were up and running – or not as the case may be – he introduced new elements to the basic formula to see what would happen.

So ... the biggest challenge he gave to the kids was the beast. It's interesting, innit, that the beast appeared in the boys' heads before it was given form by the dead parachutist. What I'm saying is that the beast is really the boys' fear and all ... all the things that go wrong on the island are 'cause of fear.

This... is bad news for the rest of us. Golding reckons that fear is what makes any group of people hostile and aggressive. Just as the boys on the island can't get on because of fear ... people in the world can't get on because of fear. It's no coincidence, is it, that the boys are stranded on the island because the adults are having a nuclear war. Er... that's it.

Make five suggestions that would improve this speech.

Score / 5

C

This is an exam preparation question.

1 **Below are some prompt cards on genetically modified foods. Unfortunately the speaker dropped the cards and they are in the wrong order. Can you rearrange them? Number the cards 1–6 to show their correct order.** (6 marks)

Genetically modified foods
what they are
how they are made
give examples – soya, tomatoes, oil seed rape
describe government trials

Advantages of genetically modified food
disease resistance
tolerance of certain weed killers – makes care of fields easier
higher yields – especially in developing countries
'better', more consistent product for consumer

My opinion
importance of scientific development
need for proper controls
need to feed the world
any questions?

Arguments for
growing world population – must do something to feed them
new and exciting technology – might have other advantages – e.g. medicinal plants
the cat is out of the bag – technology is available – somebody will use it – might as well be under controlled conditions

Problems with genetically modified foods
genetics very complicated – we don't know what full effect of modification might be
'genetic spread' – GM plants will cross fertilise with wild plants – new unintended results
cross species spread – e.g. weed-killer tolerance might spread to weeds – superweeds

Arguments against
unforeseen side-effects – things look OK in the lab but not in the real world – e.g. thalidomide
danger of superweeds, etc
just a way of making profit – GM foods are copyrighted – same companies control weed killers
other ways of increasing food yields are available

2 **Give a talk based on these notes.** (10 marks)

Score /16

For more on this topic see pages 6–29 of your Success Guide.

Total score /26

How well did you do? 0–5 Try again 6–13 Getting there 14–20 Good work 21–26 Excellent!

Speaking and listening 2

A

Different situations call for different language approaches. Match the examples of language use with the most appropriate situation.

1 **I've had enough of this. Get lost.** (1 mark)

a) colloquial speech
b) formal essay
c) informal letter
d) formal speech

2 **I often think of the time we spent together last summer.** (1 mark)

a) colloquial speech
b) formal essay
c) informal letter
d) formal speech

3 **I would be extremely grateful if you could give this matter your urgent attention.** (1 mark)

a) colloquial speech
b) formal essay
c) informal letter
d) formal speech

4 **I don't know much about art but I know what I like.** (1 mark)

a) colloquial speech
b) formal essay
c) informal letter
d) formal speech

5 **I intend to discuss the different methods of filtration used in modern sewage recycling plants.** (1 mark)

a) colloquial speech
b) formal essay
c) informal letter
d) formal speech

Score /5

B

Rewrite the following informal statements more formally.

a) If you're not sure where to go it's probably worth checking out the information desk.

....

....

b) I've always reckoned the food here was a bit iffy.

....

c) CU L8R

....

d) The film was really scary. It still gives me the creeps just thinking about it.

....

e) So she turns round to me and goes 'You leavin' now or what?' and I go 'Maybe. Depends.'

....

f) The teacher mumbled so a lot of the kids didn't get what he was saying.

....

Score /6

C

This is an exam preparation question. Answer both parts of the question. Continue on separate sheets of paper where necessary.

1 **Write the beginning of a speech aimed at teenagers in which you *argue* for guaranteed minimum pocket money.** (10 marks)

....

....

....

....

....

....

....

....

....

....

....

....

2 **Write the beginning of a speech aimed at parents in which you try to *persuade* them to give their children more pocket money.** (10 marks)

....

....

....

....

....

....

....

....

....

....

....

....

Score / 20

For more on this topic see pages 6–29 of your Success Guide.

Total score / 31

How well did you do? 0–7 Try again 8–17 Getting there 18–25 Good work 26–31 Excellent!

Original writing

A

Choose just one answer a, b, c or d.

1 Which of the following genres are not allowed in original writing? (1 mark)

a) romantic fiction
b) autobiography
c) descriptive writing
d) there are no restrictions on genre

2 In your original writing coursework you should aim for (1 mark)

a) brief accounts
b) convincing and concise writing
c) long projects
d) at least a thousand words

3 Original writing (1 mark)

a) must be completely original and not related to any other parts of the course
b) may emerge from work done in other parts of the course
c) should include some oral preparation
d) should not be based on things you have read independently

4 If you decide to submit poetry it is a good idea to (1 mark)

a) make sure it rhymes
b) write one long poem of about 1000 words
c) include a brief commentary on the poems
d) write in ballad quatrains

5 Which of the following is most important for gaining good marks in original writing? (1 mark)

a) originality
b) perfect spelling
c) varied sentence structure
d) well-focused and appropriate writing

Score /5

B

Match the following sentences to their genre.

1 Marsha hacked down the last wall of creepers and was rewarded by a sight unseen for a thousand years; the lost Temple of Uxor.

2 I was born, according to my parents, on a stormy night in November and storms have been pretty much part of my life ever since.

3 The Fleet river is one of the lost rivers of London. It still flows and it still feeds into the Thames, but very few people have actually seen it.

4 The dead man walked towards me, grinning through lips that were already starting to rot away.

5 The doctor injected the nanobots into my arm. 'Well, that should keep you fit and healthy for another seventy five years,' he said.

6 Moving through the empty spaces. Unmoved by all the empty faces.

7 I grabbed him by the neck and pushed him against the wall. He wasn't pleased. 'Just a few questions,' I said.

A Travel writing
B Science fiction
C Detective fiction
D Autobiography
E Poetry
F Horror
G Adventure

Score /14

C

This is an exercise about adding an extra chapter to a known text. Use the framework below to help you to plan your answer. Answer all parts of the question. Continue on separate sheets of paper where necessary.

Identify a gap in the story. What happened just before the events of the text? What happened after?

....

....

....

....

Which characters are involved? What do we know about them? What would we like to know?

....

....

....

....

What will you add to the text? A happier ending? More detail about a character?

....

....

....

....

What is the style of the original? How much dialogue is used? How much description? Does it use formal or informal language?

....

....

....

....

How is the original written? Long or short sentences/paragraphs. Adjectival descriptions? Similes, metaphors and other literary devices?

....

....

....

....

For more on this topic see pages 30–45 of your Success Guide.

Total score / 19

How well did you do? 0–4 Try again 5–10 Getting there 11–15 Good work 16–19 Excellent!

Personal writing

A

Choose just one answer a, b, c or d.

1 The plot of a story consists of (1 mark)

a) its main events
b) its main events and the connections between them
c) an evil plan hatched by one of the characters
d) your plan of the story before you write it

2 Which of the following is not a fiction genre? (1 mark)

a) romance
b) science fiction
c) detective
d) biography

3 The hook of a story is (1 mark)

a) the thing that it is really about
b) the twist in its tail
c) its moral or message
d) an interesting beginning

4 First person narration involves (1 mark)

a) the use of an 'I' point of view
b) only one person telling the story
c) telling the reader what goes on in the minds of the characters
d) using a single character

5 One advantage of third person narration over first person narration is (1 mark)

a) you can tell the story in different voices
b) you can give the thoughts of more than one character
c) it is less complicated than first person narration
d) it helps create suspense

Score / 5

B

Read the following paragraph from the beginning of a science fiction story and then answer the question.

I woke up and had my breakfast. I had toast
I think. Then I got up and went to the
office. As usual there was a queue waiting
for me but I tried not to notice how strange
some of them looked as I walked past them
into my office. The first alien who walked
through my door was called Adj. He was
from Alpha Centauri. He didn't have too
many eyes and moved around on two legs –
in poor light he would have passed for
human.
'Greetings!' he said. (What is it with aliens
and saying 'Greetings!'? Can't they say 'Hi'
like everybody else?)
'Hi,' I said, 'What's your problem?'
'Well,' he began …

Suggest five ways in which this story could be improved.

....

....

....

....

....

....

....

....

Score / 5

C **This is an exam preparation question. Answer all parts of the question. Continue on separate sheets of paper where necessary.**

Writing fiction

Use the following template to make notes to plan a piece of fiction.

Characters – who is involved? What are their relationships?

Main character

Other character

Setting – where does the story take place?

When? – what time period?

Genre – what kind of fiction?

Target audience – how to appeal to them?

Structure

Beginning – set up story, characters and setting. Introduce problem

Middle – problem reaches a crisis

End – problem solved

Hook – start at interesting point? Start at middle/end and then use flashback?

For more on this topic see pages 30–45 of your Success Guide.

Total score / 10

How well did you do? 0–2 Try again 3–5 Getting there 6–8 Good work 9–10 Excellent

Essay writing

A

Choose just one answer a, b, c or d.

1 A well-planned essay (1 mark)

a) has a logical structure
b) uses connectives to show how ideas are related
c) makes good use of evidence
d) addresses the key words and phrases in the question and answers them

2 Literary essays should contain (1 mark)

a) quotations
b) quotations and close references to the text
c) points backed up by quotations and comments
d) quotations and comments

3 The conclusion of an essay should (1 mark)

a) restate your arguments
b) sum up your arguments and say what has been learned
c) restate the arguments and point the way to further questions
d) give the essay a sense of finality

4 Effective use of quotations means (1 mark)

a) quoting the exact word or phrase that has lead to a conclusion
b) providing enough of a context to let the reader judge the quotation
c) choosing words and phrases that are familiar to the reader
d) commenting appropriately on a text

5 A close reference to a text is most appropriate (1 mark)

a) when you can't remember the exact quotation
b) when the actual language used by the author is not important
c) when you are making a general point
d) when there isn't time to tell the full story

Score /5

B

Read the following passage from a student's essay and then answer the questions that follow on separate paper.

The main message, then, in 'To Kill a Mockingbird' is not to judge by appearances. Scout and Jem learn that the monsters of their childhood, Boo and Mrs Dubose, have stories of their own and the town has learned, a little, that you should not judge a man by his colour. The key to all of this is sympathy for outsiders and loners; as Atticus says you should never judge someone unless you have 'walked around in his shoes'. (This message works most of the time but we shouldn't forget that Tom Robinson got into trouble for being too sympathetic.) The final part of the book, when Scout sees her own childish world from Boo's point of view, also tells us that we should try to see ourselves from other people's points of view.

1 Where do you think this passage comes from in the essay? .... (1 mark)

2 Identify a quotation. Do you think it has been used effectively? .... (2 marks)

3 Identify a close reference to the text. Do you think it has been used effectively? .... (2 marks)

4 Do you think this piece of writing works well? Give reasons for your answer. .... (2 marks)

5 Suggest one improvement to this passage. .... (1 mark)

Score /8

C

This is a GCSE-style question. Answer all parts of the question. Continue on separate sheets of paper where necessary.

Writing a literary essay

Identify one character from a novel you have studied and explain how the character is changed by his or her experiences. Use the headings below as starting points for your character analysis.

What the character is like at the beginning of the novel

....

....

....

....

The important incidents that cause a change

....

....

....

....

What the character is like at the end

....

....

....

....

How the author helps us to see and understand the change

....

....

....

....

Score / 10

For more on this topic see pages 30–45 of your Success Guide.

Total score / 23

How well did you do? 0–5 Try again 6–12 Getting there 13–18 Good work 19–23 Excellent!

The media

A

Choose the best response, a, b, c or d to the following statements and questions.

1 Which of the following is a media text? (1 mark)

a) a newspaper
b) a magazine
c) a Hollywood film
d) all of the above

2 'Bias' in the media usually means: (1 mark)

a) deliberately misleading stories
b) a tendency to report from only one point of view
c) racism or sexism
d) avoiding unpopular issues

3 In your media assignments you will have to (1 mark)

a) inform, explain, describe
b) imagine, explore, entertain
c) analyse, review, comment
d) persuade, argue, advise

4 The media are covered in (1 mark)

a) coursework only
b) exam work only
c) exam work and coursework
d) it depends on the options my teacher has chosen

5 In film work you may discuss (1 mark)

a) an entire film
b) the opening of a film
c) trailers for films
d) all of the above

Score /5

B

Below is an extract from part of a newspaper article. Read it carefully and then answer the questions that follow.

Batman Begins*****

Film review

Anyone who remembers the worst excesses of the last two Batman films might approach Christopher Nolan's latest Batman with some caution, but there is no need to worry. This is a magnificent return to form for the franchise. Christian Bale makes a suitably tortured Batman and his journey from guilt to redemption is almost entirely convincing. This is not to say that 'Batman Begins' is some sort of morality play. Nolan handles the action sequences with skill and there is a fine supporting cast in the likes of Morgan Freeman, Michael Caine and Cillian Murphy.

1 What do you think the five stars in this review show?

....

....

.... (1 mark)

2 What is the purpose of a review of this length?

....

....

.... (2 marks)

3 Explain whether you would expect a review like this to be for the film's cinema release or for its first showing on television.

....

....

.... (2 marks)

Score /5

C

This is a GCSE-style question.

Batman is an example of a comic book character who has been brought to the screen. There are many adaptations of this type.

Choose a comic book character that you know (it could be Batman) and plan the lighting and colour scheme for a key scene in the movie.

Use the space below to draw a sketch of the scene and then explain your ideas in the box. Think about how light and colour help to create the atmosphere for the scene.

Score / 10

For more on this topic see pages 30–45 of your Success Guide.

Total score / 20

How well did you do? ✗ 0–4 Try again 5–10 Getting there 11–15 Good work 16–20 Excellent! ✓

Sound

A

Choose the best response, a, b, c or d to the following statements and questions.

1 Diegetic sound is (1 mark)

a) sound that has been added by the studio
b) sound that occurs in the world of the film
c) unintended sounds on a film set
d) a brief period of 'silence on the sound track

2 A sound bridge is (1 mark)

a) a transition from diegetic to non-diegetic sound
b) a sort of segue
c) when sound from one scene carries over into another
d) a special type of sound effect

3 Which of the following would not be included in the mise-en-scene (1 mark)

a) sound effects
b) props
c) costumes
d) a character's back story

4 Which of the following would not be a reason for the director to use silence? (1 mark)

a) to create tension
b) to calm things down
c) to keep the film budget down
d) to give the audience a rest after an action scene

5 The soundtrack of a film is (1 mark)

a) all the sounds in the film together
b) a collection of music used in a film
c) the white border of a film that used to contain the sound
d) all of the above

Score / 5

B

Put the following five sounds into a logical sequence.

The wail of an alarm

The creaking as someone opens something

A crash of a breaking glass

Grunting and quiet movement

A light clicking on

....

....

....

....

....

....

Score / 5

C **This is a GCSE-style question.**

Sound tracks often contain music that is relevant to the scene. In the boxes on the left draw some scenes from a film. On the right name a piece of music and explain why it would go well with your scene

Scene	
	Title of music Explanation
	Title of music Explanation
	Title of music Explanation

Score / 15

For more on this topic see pages 30–45 of your Success Guide.

Total score / 25

How well did you do? 0–5 Try again 6–13 Getting there 14–19 Good work 20–25 Excellent!

Camera shots

A

Choose the best response, a, b, c or d to the following statements and questions.

1 An establishing shot is used to (1 mark)

a) create atmosphere
b) show the thing actually being advertised
c) show the time and place in which the ad takes place
d) create an air of respectability for the product

2 High angle shots can (1 mark)

a) make the thing viewed seem insignificant
b) be expensive to take and usually show something special
c) give a distorted view of a character
d) give the viewer a sense of perspective

3 The best shot for showing a character's emotion is a (1 mark)

a) long shot
b) pan
c) close-up
d) high-angle shot

4 Long shots (1 mark)

a) help to establish who is important
b) use up more film than short shots
c) show the head and shoulders of a character
d) have to be used sparingly in a short advertisement

5 Point of view shots (1 mark)

a) change the camera's viewing angle
b) are used when an opinion is being expressed
c) are a type of extreme close-up
d) show what a character would see

Score / 5

B

The following diagrams show different types of shots. Label each shot correctly.

1

2

3

4

5

A Close up B High angled shot C Panning shot D Long shot E Extreme close-up

Score / 5

C This is a GCSE-style question

Preparation.

Use the storyboard below to plan a brief scene in a film. Remember to use different shots, sound effects and music to make your scene as interesting as possible.

Shot	Shot	Shot
Dialogue/Voice-over/Sound	Dialogue/Voice-over/Sound	Dialogue/Voice-over/Sound
Shot	Shot	Shot
Dialogue/Voice-over/Sound	Dialogue/Voice-over/Sound	Dialogue/Voice-over/Sound
Shot	Shot	Shot
Dialogue/Voice-over/Sound	Dialogue/Voice-over/Sound	Dialogue/Voice-over/Sound

Score / 20

For more on this topic see pages 30–45 of your Success Guide.

Total score / 30

How well did you do? ✗ 0–6 Try again 7–15 Getting there 16–23 Good work 24–30 Excellent! ✓

Camera movements

A

Choose just one answer a, b, c or d.

1 Tripods are (1 mark)

a) the creatures in *The War of the Worlds*
b) a way of keeping a camera steady
c) gradually being replaced by steadicams
d) a sort of pudding that comes in three layers

2 CGI stands for (1 mark)

a) Computer Generated Images
b) Camera Generated Images
c) Computer Graphic Imaging
d) Camera Gate Inversion

3 Directors use multiple cameras nowadays (1 mark)

a) to avoid missing a special effect
b) because film and cameras are much cheaper now
c) because the restrictions on the number of camera operators per film have been lifted
d) to allow the audience to see an action from a range of view points

4 Why might a camera zoom in from a high angled shot? (1 mark)

a) to make the audience feel dizzy
b) to confuse the audience by looking at things from an odd view point
c) to give sense of a scene as a whole before picking out one or two characters
d) have to be used sparingly in a short advertisement

5 A long single take is when (1 mark)

a) the period when only one camera is filming
b) when the actors get a scene right first time
c) the camera stays with a single event without cutting away
d) the camera lingers in one place even when the action has moved on

Score / 5

B

Match the camera movements to the appropriate scene.

A A shaky camera	1 A story told by a mad person
B Long slow zoom in	2 A Western
C A static camera	3 An action scene
D A slow pan along the horizon	4 A very formal meeting
E Plenty of rapid jump cuts	5 A romantic encounter

Score / 5

C

This is a GCSE-style question.

Preparation.

1 **Use the Storyboard below to analyse a short sequence of a film. Anything from a TV ad to a feature film can be used. Choose a relatively busy section and draw a sketch of what happens. Only start a new drawing when there is a cut – a change of shot. Also jot down what is said and what you hear in each shot.**

2 **Compare your scene with a partners and discuss the effects of the different shots.**

Shot Dialogue/Voice-over/Sound	Shot Dialogue/Voice-over/Sound	Shot Dialogue/Voice-over/Sound
Shot Dialogue/Voice-over/Sound	Shot Dialogue/Voice-over/Sound	Shot Dialogue/Voice-over/Sound

Score / 20

For more on this topic see pages 30–45 of your Success Guide.

Total score / 40

How well did you do? 0–8 Try again 9–20 Getting there 21–31 Good work 32–40 Excellent!

Editing

A

Choose the best answers from the options given with each of the following questions.

1 **Film editors and newspaper editors are similar in which of the following ways?** (1 mark)

a) they are both in charge of overall production
b) they are usually the best paid members of their organisation
c) they both decide what does and does not go into the finished product
d) they both work closely with writers

2 **Continuity is** (1 mark)

a) the way a film flows from scene to scene
b) responsibility for making sure actors and scenery look the same from take to take
c) ensuring that the story makes sense to the audience
d) all of the above

3 **A jump cut is** (1 mark)

a) hardly noticeable
b) only made if there are continuity problems in a scene
c) a re-focusing of the camera within a scene
d) when one image appears from beneath another

4 **Fade outs** (1 mark)

a) always indicate the passage of time
b) sometimes indicate the passage of time
c) are used to add to the running time of a film
d) give an old-fashioned feel to a film

5 **A long single take is when:** (1 mark)

a) the period when only one camera is filming
b) when the actors get a scene right first time
c) the camera stays with a single event without cutting away
d) the camera lingers in one place even when the action has moved on

Score / 5

B

The job of a film editor is to make a film make sense and move forward at an appropriate pace.
Below are twelve shots from a film. How many can you remove without ruining the story? What is the smallest number needed?

1 **Crowd arriving outside church**
2 **Shot of vicar fussing over robes**
3 **Shot of groom looking nervous**
4 **Shot of best man looking nervous**
5 **Shot of Bride getting out of car**
6 **Shot of best man looking very nervous – pats his pockets**
7 **Bride walks up the aisle**
8 **Shot of best man extremely worried – still searching pockets**
9 **Shot of small girl noticing something**
10 **Bride arrives at the altar**
11 **Small girl picks up box with ring on it from the best man's chair**
12 **Girl gives ring to best man**

Score / 10

C

GCSE Media Coursework essay plan.

Refer to the essay plan on page 43 of the Success Guide and use the frame below to fill the details of your own essay.

Title
Paragraph 1 (Introduction)
Paragraph 2 (Stunts and special effects)
Paragraph 3 (Lighting and colour)
Paragraph 4 (Sound)
Paragraph 5 (Camera shots)
Paragraph 6 (Camera movement)
Paragraph 7 (Mise en scène)
Paragraph 8 (Editing)
Paragraph 9 (Concluding your essay)

For more on this topic see pages 30–45 of your Success Guide. Total score / 15

How well did you do? 0–6 Try again 7–9 Getting there 10–12 Good work 13–15 Excellent!

Shakespeare assignment

A

Choose just one answer a, b, c or d.

1 In his tragedies and history plays Shakespeare wrote about (1 mark)

a) the lives of ordinary men and women
b) men and women in power
c) the whole of society
d) the English royal family

2 In his comedies Shakespeare wrote about (1 mark)

a) mostly nobles
b) mostly commoners
c) mostly nobles with a few commoners
d) mostly commoners with a few nobles

3 The role of fate is most important in (1 mark)

a) tragedies
b) comedies
c) histories
d) romances

4 Shakespeare regarded self knowledge as (1 mark)

a) a subject for comedy
b) an antidote to comedy
c) very rare
d) very desirable

5 Shakespeare's comedies often involve (1 mark)

a) slapstick
b) disguise and confusion
c) surreal situations
d) thwarted ambition

Score /5

B

1 Fill in the following table as fully as you can with reference to the play you have studied.

There is no score for this exercise but it will help you to understand the structure of your play.

Act and its function	What happens
Act 1 Introduction	
Act 2 Problems revealed	
Act 3 Chaos/loss of harmony	
Act 4 Problems continue	
Act 5 Climax Harmony restored	

C

This is a coursework practice question. Answer all parts of the question. Continue on separate sheets of paper where necessary.

Writing about plot

Use the following writing frame to discuss the plot of your set play.
There are no marks for this exercise but it could be used as part of your essay preparation.

In .... the most important event as far as plot is concerned is

....

The first consequence of this event is

....

....

A further consequence is

....

....

The main character's response to the event is

....

....

Another character who is affected is

....

....

The language used at this point in the play shows

....

....

Shakespeare structures this part of the play so that

....

....

The effect on the audience of this event is

....

....

Through this event Shakespeare is able to explore the theme of

....

....

Note: You can use this frame as part of a longer essay.

For more on this topic see pages 46–59 of your Success Guide.

Total score / 5

How well did you do? ✗ 0–1 Try again 2–3 Getting there 4 Good work 5 Excellent ✓

Shakespeare's imagery

A

The following questions all use quotations from plays by Shakespeare. Choose just one answer, a, b, c or d.

1 **'Feather of lead, bright smoke, cold fire, sick health' (*Romeo and Juliet*) are examples of** (1 mark)

a) simile
b) metaphor
c) personification
d) oxymoron

2 **'Our doubts are traitors' (*Measure for Measure*) is an example of** (1 mark)

a) a simile
b) a metaphor
c) personification
d) oxymoron

3 **'Violent delights have violent ends' (*Romeo and Juliet*) is an example of** (1 mark)

a) repetition for emphasis
b) repetition for contrast
c) oxymoron
d) symbolism

4 **'She sat like patience on a monument' (*Twelfth Night*) is an example of** (1 mark)

a) a simile
b) a metaphor
c) personification
d) oxymoron

5 **'Time hath, my lord, a wallet at his back, Wherein he puts alms for oblivion' (*Troilus and Cressida*) is an example of** (1 mark)

a) a simile
b) a metaphor
c) personification
d) oxymoron

Score / 5

B

Read the following speech from *The Merchant of Venice* and answer the question that follows.

Portia: The quality of mercy is not strain'd;
It droppeth as the gentle rain from heaven
Upon the place beneath. It is twice blest:
It blesseth him that gives and him that takes.
'Tis mightiest in the mightiest; it becomes
The throned monarch better than his crown;
His sceptre shows the force of temporal power,
The attribute to awe and majesty,
Wherein doth sit the dread and fear of kings;
But mercy is above this sceptred sway,
It is enthroned in the hearts of kings,
It is an attribute to God himself;
And earthly power doth then show likest God's

What are the 'qualities of mercy' according to this extended metaphor?

....

....

Score / 5

C

This is an exam preparation question. Answer all questions.

Writing about imagery – The blood motif in *Macbeth*.
If you are not studying *Macbeth* you can apply this exercise to the play you are studying.
The word blood occurs 41 times in *Macbeth*. In the three quotations that follow we can see how Shakespeare exploits this motif as his characters develop during the play.

Macbeth with King Duncan's blood on his hands
ACT 2 SCENE 2
MACBETH:
Whence is that knocking?
How is't with me, when every noise appals me?
What hands are here? Ha, they pluck out mine eyes!
Will all great Neptune's ocean wash this blood
Clean from my hand? No, this my hand will rather
The multitudinous seas incarnadine,
Making the green one red.

Re-enter LADY MACBETH.
LADY MACBETH:
My hands are of your colour, but I shame
To wear a heart so white. ...
Retire we to our chamber.
A little water clears us of this deed.
How easy is it then! Your constancy
Hath left you unattended.

Macbeth dismisses his wife's fears
ACT 3 SCENE 4
MACBETH:
I am in blood
Stepp'd in so far that, should I wade no more,
Returning were as tedious as go o'er.

Lady Macbeth is sleep walking and talking to herself
ACT 5 SCENE 1
LADY MACBETH:
Out, damned spot! Out, I say! One – two – why then 'tis time to do't. Hell is murky. Fie, my lord, fie! A soldier, and afeard? What need we fear who knows it, when none can call our power to account? Yet who would have thought the old man to have had so much blood in him?

LADY MACBETH:
Here's the smell of the blood still. All the perfumes of Arabia will not sweeten this little hand. Oh, oh, oh!

1. **Describe Macbeth's reaction to Duncan's blood on his hands.**

2. **Describe Lady Macbeth's reaction.**

3. **How does Macbeth feel about blood half way through the play?**

4. **How has the memory of Duncan's blood affected Lady Macbeth's mental state by the end of the play?**

5. **How has Shakespeare used imagery to emphasise Lady Macbeth's change of attitude?**

Score / 10

For more on this topic see pages 46–59 of your Success Guide.

Total score / 20

How well did you do? ✗ 0–4 Try again 5–10 Getting there 11–15 Good work 16–20 Excellent! ✓

Essay notes on Caliban

A

The following questions relate to *The Tempest*. Choose just one answer, a, b, c or d.

1 Caliban is (1 mark)

a) a follower of Antonio
b) the only character native to the island
c) the son of Setebos
d) a warlock

2 Caliban's attitude to Prospero is best described as (1 mark)

a) respectful
b) disdainful
c) dismissive
d) resentful

3 The thing that Caliban has in common with Miranda is (1 mark)

a) ignorance of the wider world
b) a love of poetry
c) dislike of Prospero
d) low tolerance for alcohol

4 The thing that Caliban has in common with Antonio is (1 mark)

a) dislike of the island
b) a capacity for evil
c) respect for Prospero
d) low quality clothing

5 Caliban and Ariel both (1 mark)

a) like being Prospero's servants
b) like playing tricks
c) want to be free of Prospero
d) prefer to avoid Prospero

Score /5

B

Read the following speeches from *The Tempest* and then answer the questions that follow.

CALIBAN: All the infections that the sun sucks up
From bogs, fens, flats, on Prosper fall, and make him
By inch-meal a disease! His spirits hear me,
And yet I needs must curse. But they'll nor pinch,
Fright me with urchin-shows, pitch me i' th' mire,
Nor lead me, like a firebrand, in the dark
Out of my way, unless he bid 'em; but
For every trifle are they set upon me;
Sometime like apes that mow and chatter at me,
And after bite me; then like hedgehogs which
Lie tumbling in my barefoot way, and mount
Their pricks at my footfall; sometime am I
All wound with adders, who with cloven tongues
Do hiss me into madness.

CALIBAN: Be not afeard. The isle is full of noises,
Sounds, and sweet airs, that give delight, and hurt not.
Sometimes a thousand twangling instruments
Will hum about mine ears; and sometimes voices,
That, if I then had wak'd after long sleep,
Will make me sleep again; and then, in dreaming,
The clouds methought would open and show riches
Ready to drop upon me, that, when I wak'd,
I cried to dream again.

1 What are do these two speeches reveal about Caliban's day to day existence on the island? (2 marks)

....

....

2 How would you describe the mood and tone of the two speeches? (4 marks)

....

....

3 Show how Shakespeare's choice of words and rhythm affect the mood of the two speeches. (4 marks)

....

....

Score /10

C This is a coursework practice question.

Writing about character

Discussing any character involves five factors:

- what the character *says*
- what the character *does*
- what the other characters say *to* the character
- what they say *about* the character
- how the character changes or develops

Use these five headings to make notes on Caliban (or any other character you have studied). You may find it easier if you copy it out on to a separate landscape sheet of paper.

There are no marks for this exercise but it could be used as part of your essay preparation.

Caliban				
What he *says*	What he *does*	What the other characters say *to* him	What they say *about* him	How he changes or develops

For more on this topic see pages 46–59 of your Success Guide.

Total score / 15

How well did you do? 0–3 Try again 4–8 Getting there 9–12 Good work 13–15 Excellent!

Spidergrams

A

Choose just one answer a, b, c or d.

1 Which of the following is not suitable as a subject for a spider diagram? (1 mark)

a) discussing a theme
b) exploring a character
c) telling the story of a play or novel
d) investigating imagery

2 Before you begin a spider diagram you should (1 mark)

a) make sure you have suitable pens and paper available
b) check the key words of the question for suitable headings
c) brainstorm ideas
d) sharpen your pencils

3 What is the point of colouring in a completed spider diagram? (1 mark)

a) it looks good
b) the colour makes it easier to remember
c) the different colours are a way of grouping ideas together
d) to make it look like a map of the London tube

4 A spider diagram is a good method of planning because: (1 mark)

a) it helps you see the connections between ideas
b) it makes a memorable revision aid
c) unexpected connections sometimes come up
d) it's a more creative approach than just jotting down points

5 What use does the Boeing corporation make of spider diagrams? (1 mark)

a) planning quilts
b) teaching engineers about aircraft design
c) decorating one of its hangars
d) they produced the world's largest spider diagram for charity

Score /5

B

Study the notes below on *Macbeth* and then complete the task that follows.

1 Are the witches responsible for the tragedy of Macbeth?

Sailor speech shows that they can't directly change fate

Temptation – Use the truth against him. Thane of Cawdor greeting is true when they utter it

Temptation 2 – All three warnings are true. Just not what Macbeth expected

Effect on Macbeth – Witches not present at murder – his decision

Effect on Lady Macbeth – Letter describes meeting – she persuades Macbeth

Conclusion

Rearrange these notes as a spider diagram.
Which version is easier to follow?

Score /6

C This is an exam practice question.

Planning an essay

Use a spider diagram to plan an essay that discusses Shakespeare's presentation of the main character of the play you have studied.

Consider:

- how we are introduced to the character
- how the character changes
- key relationships
- important plot developments

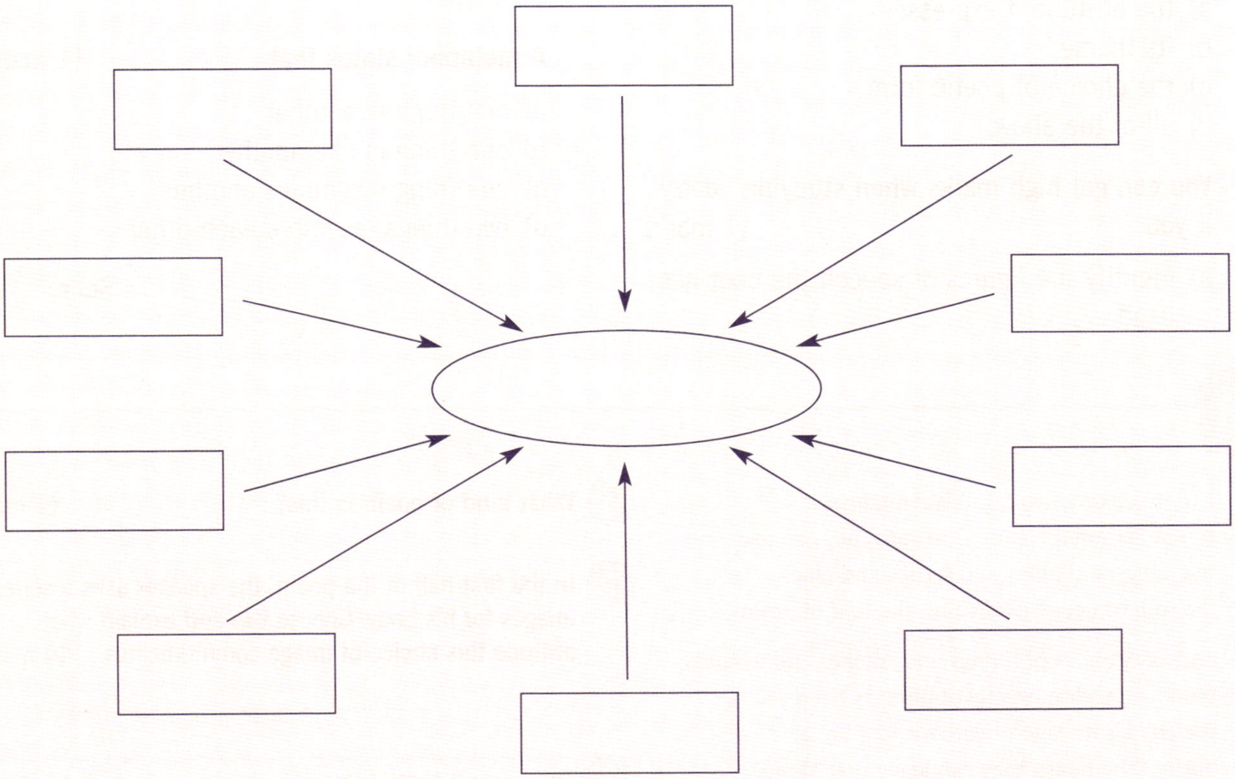

Score / 10

For more on this topic see pages 46–59 of your Success Guide.

Total score / 21

How well did you do? ✗ 0–8 Try again 9–12 Getting there 13–18 Good work 19–21 Excellent! ✓

Studying poetry

A

Choose just one answer a, b, c or d.

1 Poetry accounts for (1 mark)

a) 15% of the English marks and 30% of the literature marks
b) 15% of the English marks and 40% of the literature marks
c) 40% of the English marks and 15% of the literature marks
d) 30% of the English marks and 30% of the literature marks

2 A poem's tone is determined by (1 mark)

a) the attitude it expresses
b) its theme
c) the choice of poetic form
d) all of the above

3 You can get high marks when studying poetry if you (1 mark)

a) identify the figures of speech the poet has used
b) identify the verse form and genre of the poem
c) identify and explain the figures of speech in the poem
d) identify the areas of the poem you can empathise with

4 Which of the following is not a figure of speech? (1 mark)

a) simile
b) metaphor
c) metonym
d) diction

5 A metaphor states that (1 mark)

a) one thing is another
b) one thing is like another
c) one thing resembles another
d) two things resemble each other

Score /5

B

Read the following short poem using the advice on page 60 of your Success Guide.

I've made out a will; I'm leaving myself
to the National Health. I'm sure they can use
the jellies and tubes and syrups and glues,
the web of nerves and veins, the loaf of brains,

and assortment of fillings and stitches and wounds,
blood – a gallon exactly of bilberry soup –
the chassis or cage or cathedral of bone;
but not the heart, they can leave that alone.
They can have the lot, the whole stock:
the loops and coils and sprockets and springs and rods
the twines and cords and strands
the face, the case, the cogs and the hands,

but not the pendulum, the ticker;
leave that where it stops or hangs.

Simon Armitage

1 What kind of poem is this? (1 mark)

....

2 In the first half of the poem, the speaker uses a series of images for his body. Choose two and explain what attitude this choice of image communicates. (4 marks)

....

....

3 The second half of the poem uses a single extended metaphor for the body. What is this metaphor and what does it reveal about the speaker's view of his body? (3 marks)

....

....

4 Given the attitude expressed in the second half of the poem, why is the final line surprising? (1 mark)

....

5 Comment on the effectiveness of the imagery in this poem. (2 marks)

....

Score /11

C This is a GCSE-style question. Plan your answer here and write your response on a separate sheet of paper

Choose one other poem from the Anthology that makes interesting use of imagery. Compare it with *I've made out a will; I'm leaving myself.*

Write about:

- the images used in the two poems
- the similarities and differences between them
- which poem you found most effective

Remember to support your comments with quotations.

....

....

....

....

....

....

....

....

....

....

Score /12

For more on this topic see pages 60–75 of your Success Guide.

Total score /28

How well did you do? ✗ 0–6 Try again 7–14 Getting there 15–22 Good work 23–28 Excellent! ✓

Writing about poetry

A

Choose just one answer a, b, c or d.

1 The theme of a poem is (1 mark)

a) a recurring phrase or set of lines
b) its central message or idea
c) the general atmosphere it creates
d) the poet's intention

2 Assonance occurs in a line of poetry when (1 mark)

a) the same vowel sound is used with different consonants
b) the same sound is used at the beginning of every word
c) a deliberately jarring note is introduced
d) there is a change in the rhythm of the line

3 Identify the rhyme scheme of a Shakespearean sonnet (1 mark)

a) a b a b a b a b a b a b a b
b) a b b a a b b a a b b a a b
c) a a b b c c d d e e f f g g
d) a b a b c d c d e f e f g g

4 A quatrain is another name for (1 mark)

a) a rapid flowing rhythm
b) the first part of a poem
c) a repeated phrase or line
d) a four line stanza

5 Onomatopoeia occurs when (1 mark)

a) the words of a poem make the same sound as the one being described
b) the rhythm of the poem resembles the rhythm being described
c) the poem contains words that mimic the sound they describe
d) all of the above

Score / 5

B

Read the following poem and then answer the questions that follow.

Patrolling Barnegat

Wild, wild the storm, and the sea high running,
Steady the roar of the gale, with incessant undertone muttering,
Shouts of demoniac laughter fitfully piercing and pealing,
Waves, air, midnight, their savagest trinity lashing,
Out in the shadows there milk-white combs careering,
On beachy slush and sand spins of snow fierce slanting,
Where through the murk the easterly death-wind breasting,
Through cutting swirl and spray watchful and firm advancing,
(That in the distance! is that a wreck? is the red signal flaring?)
Slush and sand of the beach tireless till daylight wending,
Steadily, slowly, through hoarse roar never remitting,
Along the midnight edge by those milk-white combs careering,
A group of dim, weird forms, struggling, the night confronting,
That savage trinity warily watching.

Walt Whitman 1856

1 What is unusual about the verbs in this poem? (2 marks)

....

....

2 Why do you think the poem contains only one sentence? (2 marks)

....

....

3 How does this help to convey the activity of the storm? (2 marks)

....

....

4 Why are the human figures so 'dim'? (2 marks)

....

....

5 Find an example of alliteration in the poem and explain how it helps to convey the meaning of the poem. (2 marks)

....

Score / 12

C

This is a GCSE-style question.

Comparing poems

Choose one other poem from the anthology that describes a natural scene. Compare it with *Patrolling Barnegat* by filling in the gaps below.

Patrolling Barnegat and .... both describe a natural scene. *Patrolling Barnegat* describes a storm while .... describes .... *Patrolling Barnegat* attempts to convey the power of the storm whereas ....

....

The theme/idea of .... is present in both poems. For instance in *Patrolling Barnegat* the poet contrasts .... with ....

In .... the poet contrasts .... with ....

Walt Whitman's choice of language is very interesting. For instance in the line .... he shows ....

Similarly, in .... the author .... We can see this in the line ....

Walt Whitman's use of imagery is .... particularly when he describes .... as .... This gives an impression of ....

The same/opposite approach is taken by .... in the image where .... is compared to ....

The effect of this is ....

Both authors use interesting sound effects. Whitman uses .... in the line .... This gives a strong sense of ....

.... uses sound effects to show .... This is most noticeable in the line .... which gives an impression of ....

The poems' meanings are enhanced with .... An example of this in *Patrolling Barnegat* is which refers to the main idea of ....

In .... the meaning is deepened by .... which refers to the idea of ....

Both poems draw the reader's attention to ....

....

To sum up I would say that .... is the more successful poem. It shows .... and .... very clearly whereas .... is less emphatic about .... and .... Both poems are interesting but in my view ....

....

For more on this topic see pages 60–75 of your Success Guide.

Total score / 17

How well did you do? ✗ 0–3 Try again 4–9 Getting there 10–13 Good work 14–17 Excellent! ✓

Comparing poems

A

Choose just one answer a, b, c or d.

1 **Which of the following themes is not a feature of Seamus Heaney's poetry?** (1 mark)

a) nature
b) autobiography
c) exploring characters from fiction or history
d) adult – child relationships

2 **Which of the following types of poem does Carol Ann Duffy seem to prefer?** (1 mark)

a) autobiography
b) descriptive poems
c) sonnets
d) adopting a persona

3 **Gillian Clarke often writes about** (1 mark)

a) adult – child relationships
b) characters from fiction or history
c) sheep farming
d) anti-social characters

4 **Which of the following does Simon Armitage seem to like?** (1 mark)

a) exploring characters from fiction or history
b) discussing death and old age
c) adopting a persona
d) adult – child relationships

5 **Which of the following seems most popular in the pre-1914 selection?** (1 mark)

a) adopting a persona
b) sonnets
c) adult – child relationships
d) autobiography

Score / 5

B

Below are the titles of four poems. For each poem identify a theme and choose three other poems to go with it.

1 ***Patrolling Barnegat*** (5 marks)

Theme ....

Companion poems ....

....

....

2 ***Digging*** (5 marks)

Theme ....

Companion poems ....

....

....

3 ***My Last Duchess*** (5 marks)

Theme ....

Companion poems ....

....

....

4 ***On my First Sonne*** (5 marks)

Theme ....

Companion poems ....

....

....

Score / 20

C

This is a GCSE-style question.

Comparing poems

For each of the poems from the previous exercise, plan an essay on the theme you identified.

Use the grid below to make notes.

Poem 1	Poem 2
Poem 3	Poem 4

For more on this topic see pages 60–75 of your Success Guide.

Total score / 25

How well did you do? ✗ 0–5 Try again 6–13 Getting there 14–19 Good work 20–25 Excellent! ✓

ELH poems 1

A

Choose just one answer a, b, c or d.

1 When choosing poems to compare you should (1 mark)

a) pick the poems you know best
b) choose poems that have a similar structure
c) choose poems that have strong similarities or areas of contrast
d) try to guess which poems the examiners had in mind

2 You should order your discussion (1 mark)

a) chronologically
b) by starting with the one mentioned by the examiners
c) according to how much you like them
d) by areas of contrast and similarity

3 The start of your essay should (1 mark)

a) relate the poems you have chosen to the topic in the question
b) name the poems you have chosen
c) attempt to grab the examiner's attention
d) be quite short – you need to get on with the body of the essay

4 A four way comparison requires (1 mark)

a) advance planning
b) a discussion of all four poems chosen
c) a comparison of each topic four times
d) quotations from all four poems

5 Within any four poems the areas of contrast and similarity will (1 mark)

a) remain constant
b) shift according to the area under discussion
c) form a continuum
d) be summed up in the conclusion

Score / 5

B

Below is a short passage from a student's response to a question on natural imagery. Read the passage and then answer the questions.

'Storm on the Island', 'Patrolling Barnegat' and 'Inversnaid' all describe 'wild nature'. 'The Field Mouse' contains images of violence but nature itself is relatively pleasant. The poem opens with a description of the hay being cut and a pleasant smell drifting across the fields. It is human activity that disturbs things. A field mouse has been hurt by the machines and by the evening the garden is full of 'refugees' from the destruction being brought about in the fields. The mouse's fragility reminds the speaker about how delicate her own children are and, perhaps affected by the 'terrible news' on the radio, the speaker dreams of civil war. The poem is understated in spite of its serious themes. The same thing could not be said of 'Patrolling Barnegat'.

1 How does the writer link her discussion of *The Field-Mouse* with other poems? (2 marks)

....

....

2 What is her main point about the poem? (1 mark)

....

....

3 How effectively is it made? (1 mark)

....

....

4 Can you suggest any improvements to this discussion? (2 marks)

....

....

Score / 6

C

This is a GCSE-style question. Answer all parts of the question. Continue on separate sheets of paper where necessary.

Comparing poems

Continue the discussion begun in Section B.
Use the prompts to help you.

1 *Storm on the Island*

What view of nature is expressed?

How is it conveyed?

How do people fit in?

....

....

....

....

(4 marks)

2 *Patrolling Barnegat*

What view of nature is expressed?

How is it conveyed?

How do people fit in?

....

....

....

....

(4 marks)

3 *Inversnaid*

What view of nature is expressed?

How is it conveyed?

How do people fit in?

....

....

....

....

(4 marks)

Score / 12

For more on this topic see pages 60–75 of your Success Guide.

Total score / 23

How well did you do? ✗ 0–5 Try again 6–12 Getting there 13–18 Good work 19–23 Excellent! ✓

ELH Poems 2

A

Choose just one answer a, b, c or d.

1 Exam questions on poems from the English literary heritage might be on (1 mark)

a) context or theme
b) content or structure
c) technique or content
d) structure or context

2 Where are you most likely to find formal poetic techniques? (1 mark)

a) in Seamus Heaney's poems
b) in Gillian Clarkes's poems
c) in Carol Ann Duffy's poems
d) in the pre-1914 poems

3 Which of the following poets does not have a sonnet included in the Anthology? (1 mark)

a) John Clare
b) Gillian Clarke
c) William Shakespeare
d) Carol Ann Duffy

4 Which of the following is not a feature of dramatic monologues? (1 mark)

a) rhyming couplets
b) use of persona
c) implied listener
d) use of present tense

5 What do the poems discussed in the Success Guide have in common apart from the fact that they are dramatic monologues? (1 mark)

a) they are all about men
b) they are all about murder
c) they all use rhyme
d) they are all set in the past

Score / 5

B

Read 'Sonnet 130' by William Shakespeare and then answer the questions.

My mistress' eyes are nothing like the sun,
Coral is far more red, than her lips red,
If snow be white, why then her breasts are dun:
If hairs be wires, black wires grow on her head:
I have seen roses damasked, red and white,
But no such roses see I in her cheeks,
And in some perfumes is there more delight,
Than in the breath that from my mistress reeks.
I love to hear her speak, yet well I know,
That music hath a far more pleasing sound:
I grant I never saw a goddess go,
My mistress when she walks treads on the ground.
And yet by heaven I think my love as rare,
As any she belied with false compare.

1 Make a list of the things that Shakespeare's mistress is not like. (8 marks)

....
....
....
....

2 Explain how Shakespeare rescues the poem from being an insult to his mistress. (2 marks)

....
....
....

3 Who is the poem really directed at? (1 mark)

....
....
....

4 What is Shakespeare's criticism of the imagery used in love poems? (2 marks)

....
....
....

Score / 13

C

This is an exam preparation question.

'Mother, any distance greater than a single span'

Mother, any distance greater than a single span
requires a second pair of hands.
You come to help me measure windows, pelmets, doors,
the acres of the walls, the prairies of the floors.

You at the zero-end, me with the spool of tape, recording
length, reporting metres, centimetres back to base, then leaving
up the stairs, the line still feeding out, unreeling
years between us. Anchor. Kite.

I space-walk through the empty bedrooms, climb
the ladder to the loft, to breaking point, where something has to give;
two floors below your fingertips still pinch
the last one-hundredth of an inch ... I reach
towards a hatch that opens on an endless sky
to fall or fly.

Simon Armitage

This poem features a combination of the ordinary and domestic with more wide-ranging images.

1 Identify five domestic images.

.... (2 marks)

2 Identify five wide-ranging images.

.... (5 marks)

3 Who are the domestic images associated with?

.... (1 mark)

4 Who are the wide ranging images associated with?

.... (1 mark)

5 Explain the impact of the words 'Anchor. Kite.' on line 8.

.... (2 marks)

6 What do the final words of the poem reveal about the speaker's attitude to his mother?

....

.... (2 marks)

7 Comment on the way this poem expresses much of its meaning through imagery.

....

....

.... (4 marks)

Score / 20

For more on this topic see pages 60–75 of your Success Guide.

Total score / 38

How well did you do? ✗ 0–8 Try again 9–19 Getting there 20–29 Good work 30–38 Excellent! ✓

Poetry of other cultures 1

A

Choose just one answer a, b, c or d.

1 **Which of the following ideas is unlikely to be explored in your work on poems from different cultures?** (1 mark)

a) ideas about language power and dialect
b) feelings of being caught between cultures
c) belief and ritual
d) a touristic view of 'abroad'

2 **Rituals** (1 mark)

a) only take place in churches
b) are a codified way of dealing with common situations
c) are an old-fashioned way of doing something
d) are an interesting pastime

3 **Enjambment is** (1 mark)

a) a pause in a line of poetry
b) a type of rhythm
c) when the meaning of one line flows onto the next
d) a sort of improvised poetry session

4 **An elegy is** (1 mark)

a) an eight-line poem
b) a sad poem
c) a type of ballad
d) a poem in praise of a dead person

5 **Free verse uses** (1 mark)

a) rhyme
b) unrhymed lines of irregular length
c) regular stanzas but no rhyme
d) irregular lines with a set rhyme scheme

Score / 5

B

Read Imtiaz Dharker's poem 'Blessing' and answer the questions below.

Blessing

The skin cracks like a pod.
There never is enough water.
Imagine the drip of it,
the small splash, echo
in a tin mug,
the voice of a kindly god.

Sometimes, the sudden rush
of fortune. The municipal pipe bursts,
silver crashes to the ground
and the flow has found
a roar of tongues. From the huts,
a congregation: every man woman

child for streets around
butts in, with pots,
brass, copper, aluminium,
plastic buckets,
frantic hands,

and naked children
screaming in the liquid sun,
their highlights polished to perfection,
flashing light,
as the blessing sings
over their small bones.

Imtiaz Dharker

1 **How are the first two lines different from the rest of the poem?** (1 mark) ....

2 **Why do you think there are so many single syllable words in lines three to five?** (2 marks) ....

3 **There are several religious images in this poem. Can you find three of them?** (3 marks) ....

4 **Why do you think this is?** (2 marks) ....

5 **What is the purpose of the long list of utensils? How is the list organised?** (2 marks) ....

6 **Comment on the effectiveness of the phrase 'liquid sun'.** (2 marks) ....

Score / 12

C

This is a GCSE-style question. Plan your answer here and write your response on separate paper.

Comparing poems

Choose one other poem from the Cluster 1 that gives you insight into life outside England. Compare it with *Blessing*.

You should write about:

- what you learn about the other country
- the attitude of the poet
- the way in which the two poets have expressed their ideas.

Refer back to the framework on page 61 of your Success Guide to help you structure your answer

Score / 20

For more on this topic see pages 60–75 of your Success Guide.

Total score / 37

How well did you do? ✗ 0–7 Try again 8–19 Getting there 20–28 Good work 29–37 Excellent! ✓

Poetry of other cultures 2

A

Choose just one answer a, b, c or d.

1 Received Pronunciation or BBC English is (1 mark)

a) the way language is spoken by most people in England
b) the way that powerful and influential people speak
c) another way of saying 'the Queen's English'
d) a way of speaking that has to be learned – it is not natural

2 A dialect is (1 mark)

a) a version of English with its own rules, vocabulary and grammar
b) a version of English that has mistakes in it
c) Any version of English that is not spoken with a BBC accent
d) A lower status version of English

3 Which one of the following statements about accent is correct? (1 mark)

a) it is impossible to speak Standard English if you have a regional accent
b) accent is the same as dialect
c) accent describes the way Standard English is spoken in a particular area
d) people with posh accents always speak Standard English

4 Phonetic spelling is (1 mark)

a) a special way of writing used by children learning to read
b) an attempt to write words down as the sound, not as they are spelt in a dictionary
c) deliberately distorted spelling used by poets for effect
d) an ancient writing system used by the Phoenicians

5 Irony is (1 mark)

a) a way of expressing anger
b) harsh and unpleasant speech
c) the name of one of the dialects of English
d) the device of saying one thing and meaning another

Score /5

B

Read the following extract from a student's comparison of 'Unrelated incidents' and 'Half-caste', and then complete the question that follows.

I didn't find either of these poems easy to understand at first as I couldn't work out what they were saying. But when we read them aloud in class it was easier to see what the poets were getting at. I liked half-caste best because it was quite funny but unrelated incidents was just rude. When I thought about it though I realised that Tom Leonard had a point people are always making fun of other people's accents and being lairey if you don't have a posh one. But I saw the other day that even posh people are trying to get rid of their accents. Half-caste is really about racism – I don't agree with racism and I think it's a good poem because it shows that people don't think what they're saying half the time. I also liked the way john agard showed that mixing things up is a good thing. Unfortunately it reminded me of that song ebony and ivory which I hate.

1 What evidence does this text show that the writer probably doesn't speak BBC English? (2 marks)

....

....

2 How does the fact that this text is expressed in a non-Standard way affect people's opinions? (2 marks)

....

....

3 What comment does she make about social attitudes to accent? (2 marks)

....

....

4 What two good points does the text make about Half-Caste? (2 marks)

....

....

Score /8

C

This is a GCSE-style question. Plan your answer here and write your response on separate paper.

Comparing poems

Choose either *Half-Caste* or *Unrelated Incidents* and then compare your choice with *Search for my Tongue.*

You should write about:

- What each poet has to say about language
- How language affects the speaker's attitude to life
- The way in which the two poets have expressed their ideas.

Refer back to the framework on page 61 of your Success Guide to help you structure your answer.

Score / 20

For more on this topic see pages 60–75 of your Success Guide.

Total score / 33

How well did you do? ✗ 0–7 Try again 8–17 Getting there 18–25 Good work 26–33 Excellent! ✓

Novels and short stories 1

A

Choose just one answer a, b, c or d.

1 In which exam is your knowledge of your set text tested? (1 mark)

a) English
b) English Literature
c) both – it is a 'crossover' unit
d) neither – it is a coursework unit

2 Which of the following texts would NOT be suitable for an English and English literature prose study unit? (1 mark)

a) *Great Expectations* by Charles Dickens
b) *Harry Potter and the Chamber of Secrets* by J K Rowling
c) *Silas Marner* by George Eliot
d) *Treasure Island* by Robert Louis Stevenson

3 You can study texts in translation if you are prepared (1 mark)

a) to do some of the translation yourself
b) to write a letter to the exam board to have your text approved
c) to write two prose studies
d) to show that you are a native speaker of the text's language

4 H G Wells is most famous for writing (1 mark)

a) detective stories
b) historical stories
c) romances
d) science fiction stories

5 How much writing is required for a prose study? (1 mark)

a) 500 words
b) 750 words
c) 1000 words
d) none at all if you are assessed orally

Score / 5

B

Answer the question below.

1 Which of the following authors and titles are not suitable for an English and English Literature crossover prose study? Circle those that apply.

a) *The Outsider* (Novel) – Albert Camus. French. Post-1914
b) *The Catcher in the Rye* (Novel) – J D Salinger. American. Post-1914
c) *Crime and Punishment* (Novel) – Fyodor Dostoyevski. Russian. Pre-1914
d) *Paradise Lost* (Poem) – John Milton. English. Pre-1914
e) *A Christmas Carol* (Novella) – Charles Dickens. English. Pre-1914
f) *Moby Dick* (Novel) – Herman Melville. American. Pre-1914
g) *Pride and Prejudice* (Novel) – Jane Austen. English. Pre-1914
h) *Ulysses* (Novel) – James Joyce. English. Post-1914
i) *Don Quixote* (Novel) – Miguel de Cervantes. Spanish. Pre-1914
j) *Alice in Wonderland* (Children's story) – Lewis Carroll. English. Pre-1914

Score / 10

C

This is an exam preparation question.

If you have a choice of novel for your prose study you might like to consider one of the novels below. Score one mark if you know the title and one if you know the author.

Openings of famous novels

a) 'The Signora had no business to do it', said Miss Bartlett, 'no business at all. She promised us south rooms with a view close together, instead of which here are north rooms, looking into a courtyard, and a long way apart. Oh, Lucy!'

b) It was a bright cold day in April, and the clocks were striking thirteen.

c) When Farmer Oak smiled, the corners of his mouth spread till they were within an unimportant distance of his ears, his eyes were reduced to chinks, and diverging wrinkles appeared round them, extending upon his countenance like the rays in a rudimentary sketch of the rising sun.

d) It was the day my grandmother exploded.

e) It was the best of times, it was the worst of times, it was the age of wisdom, it was the age of foolishness, it was the epoch of belief, it was the epoch of incredulity, it was the season of Light, it was the season of Darkness, it was the spring of hope, it was the winter of despair, we had everything before us, we had nothing before us, we were all going direct to Heaven, we were all going direct the other way – in short, the period was so.

f) It is a truth universally acknowledged, that a single man in possession of a good fortune, must be in want of a wife.

g) No one would have believed in the last years of the nineteenth century that this world was being watched keenly and closely by intelligences greater than man's and yet as mortal as his own; that as men busied themselves about their various concerns they were scrutinised and studied, perhaps almost as narrowly as a man with a microscope might scrutinise the transient creatures that swarm and multiply in a drop of water.

h) Mr. Utterson the lawyer was a man of a rugged countenance, that was never lighted by a smile; cold, scanty and embarrassed in discourse; backward in sentiment; lean, long, dusty, dreary and yet somehow lovable.

i) There was no possibility of taking a walk that day.

j) Miss Brooke had that kind of beauty which seems to be thrown into relief by poor dress.

Score / 20

For more on this topic see pages 76–85 of your Success Guide.

Total score / 35

How well did you do? 0–7 Try again 8–18 Getting there 19–27 Good work 28–35 Excellent!

Great Expectations

A **Read the following extract that consists of the whole of Chapter 1 from 'Great Expectations' by Charles Dickens.**

My father's family name being Pirrip, and my Christian name Philip, my infant tongue could make of both names nothing longer or more explicit than Pip. So, I called myself Pip, and came to be called Pip.

I give Pirrip as my father's family name, on the authority of his tombstone and my sister – Mrs Joe Gargery, who married the blacksmith. As I never saw my father or my mother, and never saw any likeness of either of them (for their days were long before the days of photographs), my first fancies regarding what they were like, were unreasonably derived from their tombstones. The shape of the letters on my father's, gave me an odd idea that he was a square, stout, dark man, with curly black hair. From the character and turn of the inscription, 'Also Georgiana Wife of the Above,' I drew a childish conclusion that my mother was freckled and sickly. To five little stone lozenges, each about a foot and a half long, which were arranged in a neat row beside their grave, and were sacred to the memory of five little brothers of mine – who gave up trying to get a living, exceedingly early in that universal struggle – I am indebted for a belief I religiously entertained that they had all been born on their backs with their hands in their trousers-pockets, and had never taken them out in this state of existence.

Ours was the marsh country, down by the river, within, as the river wound, twenty miles of the sea. My first most vivid and broad impression of the identity of things, seems to me to have been gained on a memorable raw afternoon towards evening. At such a time I found out for certain, that this bleak place overgrown with nettles was the churchyard; and that Philip Pirrip, late of this parish, and also Georgiana wife of the above, were dead and buried; and that Alexander, Bartholomew, Abraham, Tobias, and Roger, infant children of the aforesaid, were also dead and buried; and that the dark flat wilderness beyond the churchyard, intersected with dykes and mounds and gates, with scattered cattle feeding on it, was the marshes; and that the low leaden line beyond, was the river; and that the distant savage lair from which the wind was rushing, was the sea; and that the small bundle of shivers growing afraid of it all and beginning to cry, was Pip.

"Hold your noise!" cried a terrible voice, as a man started up from among the graves at the side of the church porch. "Keep still, you little devil, or I'll cut your throat!"

A fearful man, all in coarse grey, with a great iron on his leg. A man with no hat, and with broken shoes, and with an old rag tied round his head. A man who had been soaked in water, and smothered in mud, and lamed by stones, and cut by flints, and stung by nettles, and torn by briars; who limped, and shivered, and glared and growled; and whose teeth chattered in his head as he seized me by the chin.

"O! Don't cut my throat, sir," I pleaded in terror. "Pray don't do it, sir."

"Tell us your name!" said the man. "Quick!"

"Pip, sir."

"Once more," said the man, staring at me. "Give it mouth!"

"Pip. Pip, sir."

"Show us where you live," said the man. "Pint out the place!"

I pointed to where our village lay, on the flat in-shore among the alder-trees and pollards, a mile or more from the church.

The man, after looking at me for a moment, turned me upside down, and emptied my pockets. There was nothing in them but a piece of bread. When the church came to itself – for he was so sudden and strong that he made it go head over heels before me, and I saw the steeple under my feet – when the church came to itself, I say, I was seated on a high tombstone, trembling, while he ate the bread ravenously.

"You young dog," said the man, licking his lips, "what fat cheeks you ha' got."

I believe they were fat, though I was at that time undersized for my years, and not strong.

"Darn me if I couldn't eat em," said the man, with a threatening shake of his head, "and if I han't half a mind to't!"

I earnestly expressed my hope that he wouldn't, and held tighter to the tombstone on which he had put me; partly, to keep myself upon it; partly, to keep myself from crying.

"Now lookee here!" said the man. "Where's your mother?"

"There, sir!" said I.

He started, made a short run, and stopped and looked over his shoulder.

"There, sir!" I timidly explained. "Also Georgiana. That's my mother."

"Oh!" said he, coming back. "And is that your father alonger your mother?"

"Yes, sir," said I; "him too; late of this parish."

"Ha!" he muttered then, considering. "Who d'ye live with – supposin' you're kindly let to live, which I han't made up my mind about?"

"My sister, sir – Mrs. Joe Gargery – wife of Joe Gargery, the blacksmith, sir."

"Blacksmith, eh?" said he. And looked down at his leg.

After darkly looking at his leg and me several times, he came closer to my tombstone, took me by both arms, and tilted me back as far as he could hold me; so that his eyes looked most powerfully down into mine, and mine looked most helplessly up into his.

"Now lookee here," he said, "the question being whether you're to be let to live. You know what a file is?"

Great Expectations

"Yes, sir."

"And you know what wittles is?"

"Yes, sir."

After each question he tilted me over a little more, so as to give me a greater sense of helplessness and danger.

"You get me a file." He tilted me again. "And you get me wittles." He tilted me again. "You bring 'em both to me." He tilted me again. "Or I'll have your heart and liver out." He tilted me again.

I was dreadfully frightened, and so giddy that I clung to him with both hands, and said, "If you would kindly please to let me keep upright, sir, perhaps I shouldn't be sick, and perhaps I could attend more."

He gave me a most tremendous dip and roll, so that the church jumped over its own weather-cock. Then, he held me by the arms, in an upright position on the top of the stone, and went on in these fearful terms:

"You bring me, to-morrow morning early, that file and them wittles. You bring the lot to me, at that old Battery over yonder. You do it, and you never dare to say a word or dare to make a sign concerning your having seen such a person as me, or any person sumever, and you shall be let to live. You fail, or you go from my words in any partickler, no matter how small it is, and your heart and your liver shall be tore out, roasted and ate. Now, I ain't alone, as you may think I am. There's a young man hid with me, in comparison with which young man I am a Angel. That young man hears the words I speak. That young man has a secret way pecooliar to himself, of getting at a boy, and at his heart, and at his liver. It is in wain for a boy to attempt to hide himself from that young man. A boy may lock his door, may be warm in bed, may tuck himself up, may draw the clothes over his head, may think himself comfortable and safe, but that young man will softly creep and creep his way to him and tear him open. I am a-keeping that young man from harming of you at the present moment, with great difficulty. I find it wery hard to hold that young man off of your inside. Now, what do you say?"

I said that I would get him the file, and I would get him what broken bits of food I could, and I would come to him at the Battery, early in the morning.

"Say Lord strike you dead if you don't!" said the man.

I said so, and he took me down.

"Now," he pursued, "you remember what you've undertook, and you remember that young man, and you get home!"

"Goo-good night, sir," I faltered.

"Much of that!" said he, glancing about him over the cold wet flat. "I wish I was a frog. Or a eel!"

At the same time, he hugged his shuddering body in both his arms – clasping himself, as if to hold himself together – and limped towards the low church wall. As I saw him go, picking his way among the nettles, and among the brambles that bound the green mounds, he looked in my young eyes as if he were eluding the hands of the dead people, stretching up cautiously out of their graves, to get a twist upon his ankle and pull him in.

When he came to the low church wall, he got over it, like a man whose legs were numbed and stiff, and then turned round to look for me. When I saw him turning, I set my face towards home, and made the best use of my legs. But presently I looked over my shoulder, and saw him going on again towards the river, still hugging himself in both arms, and picking his way with his sore feet among the great stones dropped into the marshes here and there, for stepping-places when the rains were heavy, or the tide was in.

The marshes were just a long black horizontal line then, as I stopped to look after him; and the river was just another horizontal line, not nearly so broad nor yet so black; and the sky was just a row of long angry red lines and dense black lines intermixed. On the edge of the river I could faintly make out the only two black things in all the prospect that seemed to be standing upright; one of these was the beacon by which the sailors steered – like an unhooped cask upon a pole – an ugly thing when you were near it; the other a gibbet, with some chains hanging to it which had once held a pirate. The man was limping on towards this latter, as if he were the pirate come to life, and come down, and going back to hook himself up again. It gave me a terrible turn when I thought so; and as I saw the cattle lifting their heads to gaze after him, I wondered whether they thought so too. I looked all round for the horrible young man, and could see no signs of him. But, now I was frightened again, and ran home without stopping.

Glossary: wittles – food. A dialect of slang form of victuals.
gibbet – a wooden structure from which executed bodies were hung.

Novels and short stories 2

A

Choose just one answer a, b, c or d.

1 Pip's full name is (1 mark)

a) Pip Philips
b) Philip Pirrip
c) Pirrip Philips
d) Pip Pirrip

2 How would you describe the atmosphere created in the second and third paragraphs? (1 mark)

a) bleak and cheerless
b) harsh and aggressive
c) sad and mournful
d) flat and monotonous

3 What is noticeable about the way the two characters speak in this extract? (1 mark)

a) Pip and Magwitch both speak in dialect
b) Pip speaks in dialect while Magwitch speaks in Standard English
c) Pip and Magwitch both speak in Standard English
d) Magwitch speaks in dialect while Pip speaks in Standard English

4 What does Magwitch's behaviour suggest? (1 mark)

a) that he is extremely cruel
b) that he is afraid of his friend
c) that he is starving
d) that he likes scaring people

5 What is the purpose of the dialogue in this chapter? (1 mark)

a) to make the story telling vivid and realistic
b) to demonstrate the power relationships between the two characters
c) to show Magwitch's intelligence but lack of education
d) all of the above

Score / 5

B

Answer the following questions based on the passage.

1 In paragraph three, that starts 'Ours was the marsh country …', how many times does Dickens use the phrase 'and that'? (1 mark)

. . . .
. . . .

2 Why do you think Dickens used this long list instead of placing the information in separate sentences? (2 marks)

. . . .
. . . .

3 In paragraph five Dickens uses another long list to describe Magwitch. (2 marks)

a) How does the list change as it progresses?

. . . .
. . . .

b) Why do you think there are so many verbs in the latter part of the list? (2 marks)

. . . .
. . . .

c) How do all these verbs affect our impression of Magwitch? (1 mark)

. . . .
. . . .

4 Identify formal and informal features of Magwitch's speech beginning 'You bring me, to-morrow morning early …' What does the speech tell us about Magwitch's intelligence? (4 marks)

. . . .
. . . .

5 In the final paragraph Magwitch is associated with a corpse coming temporarily back to life. What does this add to our impression of him at this point? (2 marks)

. . . .
. . . .

Score / 14

C

This is a coursework practice question.

Coursework: Explore Chapter One as an introduction to *Great Expectations*.

You can use the following essay plan to help you to submit a piece of coursework on *Great Expectations* or you can study the plan to help you with work on a different novel.

Essay plan:
You should write **at least** a paragraph on each of the following issues:

Setting and atmosphere
- Select elements of the setting and explain the atmosphere and mood created. Make sure you mention the types of images used (if they are symbols, personification, metaphors, etc.) and explain their effect.
- How does this atmosphere prepare us for the novel as a whole?

The character of Pip
- What is our initial impression of him? Think about character traits he seems to display.
- How does this prepare for his actions later in the novel?

The character of Magwitch
- What is our initial impression of him?
- Make sure you mentioned things that suggest he is bad/not to be admired, and also elements that make us pity him.
- How does this introduction prepare us for his actions later in the novel?
- How does the final image of Magwitch as a corpse on temporary leave from the gibbet prepare us for Magwitch's fate at the end of the novel?

Dialogue, dialect and power
- How does the structure of the dialogue demonstrate the power relationship between the two characters?
- What is the importance of the fact that Magwitch uses dialect and that Pip does not?
- How do these words prepare for or contrast with their later relationship?

Themes
- What does the chapter suggest about at least **three** of these key themes?
  - Childhood – what sort of experience is childhood in this chapter, why? How about the experience of childhood (by Pip and others) in the book as a whole?
  - Money – how are wealth and poverty presented in this chapter and in the book as a whole? (i.e. good or bad?)
  - Crime – what is our initial impression of crime in the novel? How does this develop later on? (Think about which characters commit crimes in terms of the law, and other types of crimes committed in the novel.)
  - Love – is there any love in this chapter? Does this tally with the rest of the book? (Try to think of any characters who experience love positively.)
  - Class/snobbery – Is there a class gap in this chapter? What about between them later in the novel? Why is this ironic? What does the whole novel suggest about snobbery?
  - Family – is there any sign of a functional family life at this stage of the novel? Are any families functional later in the novel? What is Dickens' overall message about families? Can you think of any that *are* functional?

For more on this topic see pages 76–85 of your Success Guide. Total score / 19

How well did you do? 0–4 Try again 5–10 Getting there 11–15 Good work 16–19 Excellent!

Literary technique 1

A

Choose just one answer a, b, c or d.

1 Round characters (1 mark)

a) have symbolic significance
b) grow and develop during the course of a novel
c) are those characters that are seen from more than one point of view
d) are a bit like Mr Men characters

2 Dialogue is used in novels and short stories (1 mark)

a) to break up long passages of description
b) because it can reveal how characters think
c) because it can be vivid and realistic
d) to make novels more like plays

3 You should pay attention to the names of characters in novels because (1 mark)

a) otherwise you will get confused
b) they sometimes provide clues about how the character will act
c) they sometimes have symbolic significance
d) authors think long and hard before naming their characters

4 A major disadvantage of using a first person narrator is: (1 mark)

a) that they can have a limited point of view
b) the reader has to trust them to tell the story
c) there is no suspense as you always know they will survive to tell the story
d) they can be irritating if you don't sympathise with them

5 A major disadvantage of using an omniscient narrator is: (1 mark)

a) they know too much and tend to appear in longer books
b) they are less realistic than first person narrators
c) they are more likely to digress
d) they are less reliable than first person narrators

Score /5

B

Read the passage below and then answer the questions that follow.

Marley was dead: to begin with. There is no doubt whatever about that. The register of his burial was signed by the clergyman, the clerk, the undertaker, and the chief mourner. Scrooge signed it: and Scrooge's name was good upon 'Change, for anything he chose to put his hand to. Old Marley was as dead as a door-nail.

Mind! I don't mean to say that I know, of my own knowledge, what there is particularly dead about a door-nail. I might have been inclined, myself, to regard a coffin-nail as the deadest piece of ironmongery in the trade. But the wisdom of our ancestors is in the simile; and my unhallowed hands shall not disturb it, or the Country's done for. You will therefore permit me to repeat, emphatically, that Marley was as dead as a door-nail.

Scrooge knew he was dead? Of course he did. How could it be otherwise? Scrooge and he were partners for I don't know how many years. Scrooge was his sole executor, his sole administrator, his sole assign, his sole residuary legatee, his sole friend and sole mourner. And even Scrooge was not so dreadfully cut up by the sad event, but that he was an excellent man of business on the very day of the funeral, and solemnised it with an undoubted bargain.

A Christmas Carol Charles Dickens

1 What is surprising about the first sentence of this story? (1 mark)

....

....

2 How well do these opening paragraphs set up a mood or tone for the story? (2 marks)

....

....

3 How would you describe the tone? (1 mark)

....

....

4 What does the digression about door-nails tell us about the story-teller? (2 marks)

....

....

5 What conclusion about Marley's life does the third paragraph lead to? (2 marks)

....

Score /8

C This is an exam preparation question.

Analysing a novel or short story

Look at the opening few paragraphs of the novel you have been studying for GCSE.

Make notes on the topics mentioned in the spaces below.

Does it introduce the major characters? If so, how?
What description does the author give of the setting?
What indication is there of the themes that are to follow?
What plot developments are indicated?

Now write a brief paragraph that describes how well the opening of your novel works as an introduction to plot, character, setting and theme.

....

....

....

....

....

....

....

....

....

....

For more on this topic see pages 76–85 of your Success Guide.

Total score / 13

How well did you do? ✗ 0–3 Try again 4–7 Getting there 8–10 Good work 11–13 Excellent! ✓

Literary technique 2

A

Choose just one answer a, b, c or d.

1 Novels can contain (1 mark)

a) a moral and a theme but not both
b) only one theme
c) more than one theme
d) only one moral

2 A motif is (1 mark)

a) a word or phrase that appears at the front of a novel
b) a recurring word, idea or image
c) a crucial moment in the plot
d) the reason why characters behave as they do

3 Novels generally use (1 mark)

a) fewer literary devices than poems
b) more literary devices than poems
c) the same kinds of literary devices as poems but over more pages
d) a different set of literary devices from poems

4 One of the most significant literary differences between novels and short stories is (1 mark)

a) short stories are shorter
b) short stories usually focus on a single incident or point in time
c) short stories use more literary devices
d) short stories have a sting in the tail

5 Short stories are probably less popular than novels because (1 mark)

a) they have fewer characters
b) dialogue tends to be fragmented
c) they are too intense
d) people like to 'get lost' in novels

Score /5

B

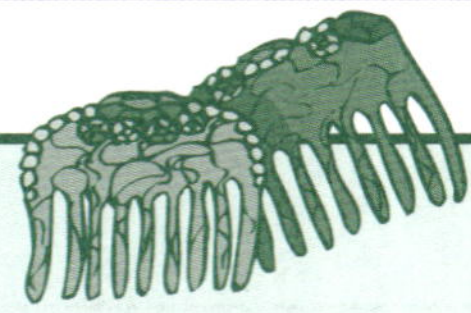

Read the passage below and then answer the questions that follow.

The passage is from near the end of a short story called 'The Gift of the Magi'. Two young people who are very poor but very much in love have sold their most precious possessions to buy gifts for each other.

For there lay The Combs – the set of combs, side and back, that Della had worshipped long in a Broadway window. Beautiful combs, pure tortoise shell, with jewelled rims – just the shade to wear in the beautiful vanished hair. They were expensive combs, she knew, and her heart had simply craved and yearned over them without the least hope of possession. And now, they were hers, but the tresses that should have adorned the coveted adornments were gone.

But she hugged them to her bosom, and at length she was able to look up with dim eyes and a smile and say: 'My hair grows so fast, Jim!'

And then Della leaped up like a little singed cat and cried, 'Oh, oh!'

Jim had not yet seen his beautiful present. She held it out to him eagerly upon her open palm. The dull precious metal seemed to flash with a reflection of her bright and ardent spirit.

'Isn't it a dandy, Jim? I hunted all over town to find it. You'll have to look at the time a hundred times a day now. Give me your watch. I want to see how it looks on it.'

Instead of obeying, Jim tumbled down on the couch and put his hands under the back of his head and smiled.

'Dell,' said he, 'let's put our Christmas presents away and keep 'em a while. They're too nice to use just at present. I sold the watch to get the money to buy your combs. And now suppose you put the chops on.'

O Henry

1 What has Della sold to buy the watch chain? (1 mark)

....

2 What has Jim sold to buy the combs? (2 marks)

....

3 What is the problem for both of them? (2 marks)

....

4 How would you describe the tone of this story? (1 mark)

....

5 Do you think this makes a good ending to a short story? Give two reasons. (2 marks)

....

Score /8

C

This is an exam preparation question.

Analysing a short story

Choose a story from the Anthology that you think has an effective ending.

Use the spaces below to make notes on the topics mentioned.

Does it resolve the 'problem' of the story?
Does it provide a satisfactory conclusion for the character/s?
Does it bring the themes of the story into focus?
Does it leave you with something to think about?

Now write a paragraph that explains the effectiveness of the ending you have chosen.

....

....

....

....

....

....

....

....

....

Score / 20

For more on this topic see pages 76–85 of your Success Guide.

Total score / 33

How well did you do? 0–3 Try again 4–7 Getting there 8–10 Good work 11–13 Excellent!

Short stories

A

Choose just one answer a, b, c or d.

1 The stories in the AQA Anthology have the following in common (1 mark)

a) they are all about children
b) they are all about parents and children
c) they are all about change
d) they all have first person narrators

2 The most popular areas for comparison of short stories are (1 mark)

a) by character and theme
b) plot and sub plot
c) plot and character
d) theme and plot

3 In the exam (1 mark)

a) you can always choose which stories you will write about
b) you can sometimes choose which stories you will write about
c) you will have no choice about which stories you will write about
d) you will always choose at least one story

4 You need to revise all of the stories before the exam because (1 mark)

a) in some years there will be no free choice of stories
b) you may want to refer to them in your essay
c) it is good revision practice
d) all the stories are interesting

5 A question on style would probably involve (1 mark)

a) discussing the authors' plot devices
b) exploring such things as narrative technique, imagery and symbolism
c) a close examination of the differences between characters
d) a discussion of how well the authors planned their stories

Score /5

B

Read and compare the two opening paragraphs of short stories from the Anthology below and then answer the questions that follow.

Your Shoes – Michèle Roberts
I thought I knew you as well as I know this house. No secret places, no hidey holes. Nothing in you I couldn't see. Now I realise how you kept yourself from me, how I didn't really know you at all.

Growing Up – Joyce Cary
Robert Quick, coming home after a business trip, found a note from his wife. She would be back at four, but the children were in the garden. He tossed down his hat, and still in his dark business suit, which he disliked very much, made at once for the garden.

1 What is the mood of *Your Shoes*? .... (1 mark)

2 How is it established? .... (2 mark)

3 What is the mood of *Growing Up*? .... (1 mark)

4 How is it established? .... (2 mark)

5 What is the difference between the narrative points of view of the two stories? .... (2 marks)

6 How well do they lead into the rest of the stories? .... (1 mark)

Score / 9

C

This is a GCSE-style question. Plan your answer here and continue your response on separate sheets of paper.

Comparing short stories

Your Shoes is an 'internal monologue', whereas *Growing Up* consists of a great deal of external dialogue. What are the advantages and disadvantages of these two methods of story telling?

Score / 20

For more on this topic see pages 76–85 of your Success Guide.

Total score / 34

How well did you do? 0–7 Try again 8–17 Getting there 18–26 Good work 27–34 Excellent!

Exam technique

A

Choose just one answer a, b, c or d.

1 Which of the following is not a useful revision technique? (1 mark)

a) working with a friend
b) setting aside a whole day for each subject
c) working to a timetable
d) brainstorming essay plans

2 How many times should you read passages in exams? (1 mark)

a) once, making notes as you go
b) once to make maximum use of the time
c) twice – first to get the general meaning and then to collect evidence
d) twice – first to get the general meaning and second as a safety check

3 In an exam essay (1 mark)

a) a full introduction is essential
b) introductions are unnecessary
c) brief introductions are advisable
d) the introduction should fully outline the rest of the essay

4 The marks for each question shown on the exam paper (1 mark)

a) should be used as guidance on the length of your answer
b) are for examiners' use only
c) tell you how many points you must make
d) can show you whether part of an answer is important or not

5 If a question asks you to 'explain', you should (1 mark)

a) present a logical argument
b) use persuasive language
c) write in Standard English
d) give a detailed account

Score /5

B

In the Western world being a vegetarian is usually a matter of choice. As a joke some vegetarians say that they eat vegetables not because of sympathy for animals but because they really hate plants. Some people are vegetarians because of their religious beliefs, but most people choose to become vegetarians because of their ideas about animals. The thought that a living, breathing, feeling creature has to be murdered just so that people can eat is too much for most vegetarians. They think that the killing of helpless animals is both unnecessary and unfair.

As the world's population increases and the world's energy supplies diminish, the production of meat for food is becoming unacceptably expensive and inefficient. A kilo of beef, for instance, is TEN TIMES more expensive to produce than a kilo of wheat. Meat production also uses up more energy than it produces. The most energy efficient meat farming gives an energy return of only 34.5 per cent whereas even the least energy efficient plant food gives a return of 328 per cent.

1 What kind of text is this? (1 mark)

....

....

2 Write down one fact and one opinion from this passage. (2 marks)

....

....

3 What methods are used to persuade in the first paragraph? (2 marks)

....

....

4 What methods are used to persuade in the second paragraph? (2 marks)

....

....

5 Identify one typographical feature used to add emphasis in this passage. (1 mark)

....

....

Score /8

C This is a GCSE-style question. Answer one question on a separate sheet of paper.

The following are the type of questions might appear in the writing section of your exam. Choose **one** and spend an hour writing a response.

1 Write an article for a teenage magazine in which you **argue** the case *either* for *or* against vegetarianism.

2 A friend is thinking of becoming a vegetarian.

Either Write a letter in which you try to **persuade** your friend to become a vegetarian.

Or Write a letter in which you try to **dissuade** your friend from becoming a vegetarian.

3 People sometimes complain that vegetarian meals can be boring.

Write an article for the cookery section of a magazine that instructs readers on how to cook an interesting and appetising vegetarian meal.

Score / 18

For more on this topic see pages 76–85 of your Success Guide.

Total score / 31

How well did you do? 0–10 Try again 11–18 Getting there 19–24 Good work 25–31 Excellent!

GCSE Practice paper 1

Text 1

bRing bRing

your old mobile to Oxfam

Why recycle mobile phones?

Apart from the fact that old handsets can be used to raise funds for Oxfam's humanitarian work around the world, donating old mobile phones to Oxfam is good because they can be recycled. Mobiles should not be disposed of thoughtlessly, because the batteries contain dangerous chemicals and because many of the materials in the phone can be reused. The most harmful chemicals in the batteries are heavy metals, such as nickel and lithium, which are toxic and not biodegradable. Buried deep in the earth, these metals could, in the future, seep into underground rivers and other water sources. Surprisingly though, the law still allows for them to be disposed of in landfill sites. Phones donated to Oxfam are refurbished and sold, raising money for our work overseas. Many of them will eventually be exported to regions with expanding mobile phone networks. These second-hand phones are usually more affordable for people there than new ones would be. The few batteries and phones which cannot be reused are sent for reprocessing, so that toxins are extracted and any materials left are reused.

Oxfam's **Bring Bring** appeal will help protect the environment, as well as benefiting people in developing countries.

did you know...?

...The batteries in your phone contain toxic heavy metals such as nickel and lithium

The mobile phone revolution

The first mobile phones were produced in the USA in the late 1970s, but they were heavy and unreliable. Mobile phones as we know them now appeared in the mid-1990s, and since then, they have grown enormously in popularity and have changed the way we communicate. It is now possible to speak to people in remote corners of the world where normal telephone technology is relatively undeveloped – or perhaps non-existent. A new form of communication has come into existence: the txt msg. This is particularly popular in some European countries, including the UK and Finland. Almost one billion text messages are sent each month in the UK.

did you know...?

...The peak hours for text messaging are between 10.30pm and 11.00pm Mobile Data Association website

What is a mobile phone made of?

A mobile phone is a technological miracle. Thirty years ago, you would have needed a whole room for this equipment. Today, it fits inside the handset. A mobile phone consists of seven main parts:

- circuit board containing several computer chips
- antenna
- liquid crystal display
- microphone
- keyboard
- speaker
- battery

In effect, a mobile phone is a type of two-way radio.

brng yr old mbl 2 Oxfm – U know it mks snse

Photo: Brian Moody

Oxfam

Activities

Here are some ways of taking your thoughts further

1 Prepare an assembly on mobile phones in order to raise money for Oxfam and to get your fellow pupils thinking about the way we communicate.

2 Is it important for everyone to have access to technology? What disadvantages do people suffer if they don't have access to the internet, e-mail, or mobile phones, or if they haven't learned how to use the technology? Should governments give computers to poorer people? Should we in the industrialised world provide technology for people in the developing world? Write a piece about your thoughts on these issues.

3 Try and find out about the way people communicate in other countries, and the way people communicated in the past. Talk to your teacher about how to make contact with people abroad. It is often better to communicate with people in developing countries by letter or fax (e-mails can be difficult for them to receive, because they take a long time to download). You could also think of the books you've read that are set in the past.

4 Rewrite a well-known story, showing how events would have turned out if mobile phones had been available. (For example, Cinderella texts her fairy godmother when her sisters have gone to the ball...use your imagination.)

5 Make a leaflet giving advice to young people about making the best use of their mobile phones. You could include tips on not spending too much money on calls, taking health precautions, communicating in other ways (face to face, letters, etc), staying safe from bullies and muggers, as well as some of the plus points of the phones (staying in contact with your friends, easy access to information, etc).

6 Draw up a cost–benefit sheet for a mobile phone. Make a list of all the costs involved on one side, and all the benefits that people get from the phone on the other. Are there any 'social costs' (eg health risks)? Is it worth the money? What might people have to do without in order to afford a phone?

Useful resources

How your phone works

Encarta Encyclopedia:
http://encarta.msn.co.uk
(search under 'Cellular Radio Telephone')

How Stuff Works:
www.howstuffworks.com/cell-phone.htm

Inventors:
http://inventors.about.com/library/weekly/aa070899.htm

Issues about phones, and phones around the world

http://news.bbc.co.uk *(search for 'mobile phone')* or search for 'mobile phone' on the site of any reputable newspaper or periodical.

Texting

www.text.it

For extra materials and worksheets connected with Oxfam's **Bring Bring** scheme, visit www.oxfam.org.uk/coolplanet. Cool Planet also features information and activities for young people and resources and ideas for teachers.

For further information about resources for schools which bring a global dimension to life in the classroom, send for a copy of Oxfam's catalogue *Oxfam Education Resources for Schools.*

Contact
Oxfam Supporter Services,
274 Banbury Road, Oxford OX2 7DZ

Tel: (01865) 312610

e-mail: oxfam@oxfam.org.uk

hndover yr hndst!

Photo: Brian Moody

Oxfam

Text 2

Saturday October 19, 2002 • *The Guardian*

What's your poison?

Many gadgets contain nasty chemicals and will never biodegrade. So, can we covet them and love the environment, too? Oliver Bennett investigates

The concept of "planned obsolescence" created a huge stir when it was first identified by Vance Packard in his 1960 book *The Waste Makers*. Packard's theory was that manufacturers designed products to have a short life, thereby committing us to a constant cycle of consumption.

Four decades on, we are in the age of junk electronics as never before. Today's technology is so transient it goes from shelf to bin in a matter of months. The average computer is changed every two years, the typical mobile phone every 18 months. Two million televisions are trashed every year. Yet, the pressure to buy new stuff is enormous – What! You haven't got a digital widescreen TV yet? Loser!

While the idea of being a responsible consumer is nice in principle, many of us are too wedded to buying the latest gadgets. Mike Childs, a senior campaigner at Friends Of The Earth, understands this human instinct to acquire, but reckons that we need to resist it. "We should step back and ask ourselves: what are the implications of buying these things?" he says. If buy we must, then manufacturers should design hardware that "can be upgraded rather than changed" and be penalised if they do not "design out waste".

Some companies are taking note. Honda and Toyota have adopted a catch-all recycling strategy known as "zero waste" – something also practised by New Zealand, the cities of Canberra and Toronto and some UK local authorities, such as Bath and North East Somerset Council.

But what about us lowly punters? There are few options for what to do with old technology. It's often not worth repairing, and anyway, there are few repairers left. The second-hand market has crashed: schools and charity shops have been inundated. So old equipment gathers dust in lofts and cupboards, in what Sarah Bond, of recycling company Shields Environmental, calls "home landfill".

We are caught between two stools. On one hand, waste directives mean that we now can't dump certain items, even if we wanted to: old televisions and PCs are now proscribed as potentially hazardous, each bearing a kilo or two of lead. Yet, on the other hand, there isn't a systematic route for responsible disposal.

Coming soon, though, is the Waste Electrical and Electronic Equipment (WEEE) Directive, due to pass through the European Parliament by 2004. This will oblige manufacturers and retailers to take back for recycling all the TVs, stereos, *et al*, they've sold.

And, slowly, things are beginning to happen here. For example, Shields Environmental recently launched Fonebak, a mobile phone recycling scheme, where you send in dud phones or take them back to a participating store. Fifteen million mobiles are replaced each year in the UK, each with the potential to leach nasty contaminants. "The worst ones are the old 'bricks'," says Sarah Bond. "A battery from one of these is enough to pollute 600,000 litres of water with cadmium." With Fonebak, metals are extracted and re-deployed; some phones are "remanufactured" to sell in developing countries; and casings are incinerated for power supply.

In tiny ways, we can already prevent gadget waste. There are several places to buy eco-friendly electronics (see left). Mainstream companies are getting in on the act, too. Consumers can choose solar-powered gizmos – calculators, radios, watches; or they can use rechargeable and recycled batteries. Panasonic uses lead-free solder; Sony has " greened" its latest Walkman/radio with decomposable "plastic" made from corn. There's even a growing range of green gimmicks: clockwork torches, clocks powered by potatoes and mouse mats made of recycled tyres.

Will this create a new glut of eco-friendly junk? Possibly. But at least today's wastemakers will have to be more responsible than those before.

From http://www.guardian.co.uk/weekend/story/0,3605,813517,00.html

1 Read the Oxfam leaflet.

You are being asked to follow an argument, select material appropriate to a purpose and tell the difference between fact and opinion.

a) Write down one opinion from page one of the leaflet.

....

.... **(2 marks)**

b) Write down one fact from the main text of the leaflet.

....

.... **(2 marks)**

c) How does the leaflet use facts to persuade people to recycle their mobiles?

....

....

....

(6 marks)

Score / 10

2 Now read the article from *The Guardian* 'What's your poison?'

Explain in your own words some of the things that ordinary people can do to increase the recycling of consumer products.

(6 marks)

Score / 6

3 You are now being asked to read the texts as media texts.

a) What do the text and images chosen for this leaflet tell you about its target audience?

(4 marks)

b) What features of the layout and presentation of the leaflet help it to reach its target audience?

(4 marks)

c) What techniques does the newspaper article use to get and hold its readers' attention?

(3 marks)

Score / 11

GCSE Practice paper 2

Text 2

What is Britishness anyway?

Apart from the sea, what keeps the British together?

David Blunkett has named academic Professor Sir Bernard Crick as the man who will set up a controversial "Britishness" test for would-be immigrants. Part of the problem might be there are so many definitions of what "Britishness" is.

Mr Blunkett's plans for citizenship tests – and his plain speaking approach on immigration and race – have led to accusations of borderline racism from some on the left.

He was warned when the tests were announced that his comments could be exploited by racists, and he has been criticised for showing a "distinct lack of understanding".

It's an illustration of how delicate a subject race still is.

Views on best of Britishness

Sophie Dahl: "Earl Grey and John Galliano"

Elton John: "Sense of humour"

Andrew Motion: "Beer on tap"

Norman Cook: "Most people speak your language when you go abroad"

Denise Lewis: "Gin and tonic"

Many have tried to define what it means to be British, sometimes in relation to race but often at the level of the constituent parts of the United Kingdom.

For former Tory chairman Norman Tebbit, it was the infamous "cricket test" which mattered. Immigrant communities, he said, should support England even when it was playing their country of origin. Many objected to having their loyalties called into question.

Commenting on Professor Crick's appointment, Lord Tebbit told BBC News Online the "cricket test" was "not a test of Britishness it was a test of integration".

"Nobody used to talk about Britishness in the 1940s and 1950s, it is a phenomenon of large numbers of non-British people coming into the country.

"The question is about foreigners and how foreigners are persuaded to adopt British customs and styles."

He said England cricket captain Nasser Hussain – who was born in India – was a good example of racial integration.

'Long shadows on county grounds'

Lord Tebbit went on: "My father's family came to Britain in the 16th Century, but I regard the Anglo-Saxon period, King Alfred and William the Conqueror are part of my inheritance."

He said the challenge will be to "persuade these people (immigrants) that Waterloo, Trafalgar and the Battle of Britain, are part of their heritage."

John Major also attempted to define Britishness, although more in an attempt to reassure those worried at EU influence than immigration.

He said that in 50 years' time, it would still be the country of "long shadows on county grounds, warm beer, invincible green suburbs, dog lovers and pools fillers and – as George Orwell said 'old maids bicycling to holy communion through the morning mist'."

Same hymn sheet?

David Blunkett mentioned two things in particular – forced marriages and genital mutilation – which he said were certainly not part of Britishness.

But stating in any detail what are characteristic of Britishness is a challenging task.

Would there, for instance, be cultural harmony in a massive jamming session between a garage collective, a colliery band, drumming Orangemen, and a chamber orchestra – all of them distinctly British in their own way?

Finding the common ground which defines a nation is a challenge for many countries, especially as the concept of the "nation state" comes into question from the rise of international bodies and multi-national companies.

Roots

Within the UK, devolution in Scotland, Wales and Northern Ireland, inspired much soul-searching about what – if anything – it meant to be British. As the devolved assemblies settle in, there are also moves for the English regions to have more autonomy.

What exemplifies Britishness? In a recent survey, 91% said it was the NHS. The concept of modern Britain was founded in 1707 with the Act of Union which brought England and Scotland together.

In just over five years' time, it will in a sense be Britain's 300th anniversary. But it may well be that without a greater sense of what constitutes Britishness, any celebrations will struggle to be a success in the public's mind.

From http://news.bbc.co.uk/1/hi/uk/1701843.stm

1 **Read the UKTV advertisement.**

You are being asked to follow an argument, select material appropriate to a purpose and tell the difference between fact and opinion.

a) Write down one statement that relates to people's opinions about the UK.

....

....

.... **(3 marks)**

b) Write down one statement that relates to facts about people from the UK.

....

.... **(3 marks)**

c) How does the advertisement use stereotypes to encourage people to identify themselves as being from the UK.

....

.... **(3 marks)**

Now read the article from BBC web page. 'What is Britishness anyway?'

d) Use your own words to explain three opinions about what it is to be British used in the body of the page.

....

....

....

....

.... **(6 marks)**

2 You are now being asked to read the texts as media texts.

a) Why do you think that the advertisers chose a combination of a dinosaur and two old ladies as the main image for this ad? How does the image reinforce the message of the text?

....

....

.... **(4 marks)**

b) Explain how this advertisement is attempting to establish a brand rather than advertising a particular product.

....

....

.... **(4 marks)**

c) What techniques does the web page article use to get and hold to 'add value' to the main article. How effective are these techniques?

....

....

.... **(4 marks)**

Score / 27

GCSE model answers – PAPER 1

1 a) 'A mobile phone is a technological miracle' or 'U know it mks snse' **(2 marks)**

b) Any fact apart from the ones in 'did you know?' boxes will do. For instance 'The first mobile phones were produced in the US in the seventies.' **(2 marks)**

c) The leaflet uses facts to persuade people to recycle their mobiles in several ways. First of all it points out that not to recycle your phone is bad for the environment. It then goes on to tell the reader how mobile phones have made people's lives better in the developed world. The leaflet assumes that the readers will be interested in mobiles and so it provides simple information about how mobile phones work. On the second page of the leaflet the facts relate more closely to Oxfam and its role in the developing world. The leaflet covers three main points in this section: how difficult communication was before mobiles; how mobiles have improved people's lives; and how mobiles help in disaster relief. In addition to all of this information the leaflet is decorated with 'did you know? boxes' that are filled with less relevant but quite interesting pieces of information. The leaflet is trying to persuade people to recycle their mobile phones either to raise money for Oxfam or so the phones can be reused in the developing world. All the information provided helps the reader to understand why this idea 'mks snse'. **(6 marks)**

2 First of all we should buy hardware that can be upgraded rather than having to be replaced or choose products that have a 'zero waste' policy. Two things that used to be sensible were repairing things rather than throwing them away and giving things to charity. Unfortunately there are few repairers left and schools and charities have too much to sell nowadays. We can use a service like 'Fonebak' to recycle mobile phones and prevent them from harming the environment. We can also choose solar-powered calculators, radios or watches or use rechargeable and recycled batteries. Finally we can buy 'green' products like clockwork torches, potato powered clocks or mouse mats made from recycled tyres. **(6 marks)**

3 a) This leaflet is obviously aimed at a young audience; the sort of people who use and are interested in mobile phones. The leaflet is meant to be friendly and informal – you can tell this from the style of typography used in the title – it looks like something a young person might produce with a marker pen. The title is also meant to be a joke as 'bring bring' is what the leaflet is asking people to do and it is also the noise made by some phones. The information in the leaflet is quite serious but it is presented in short bursts so as not to put people off. Also there are little pieces of trivia in the 'did you know?' boxes that help to maintain interest. Although the audience is young people the leaflet does not patronise its audience by being too simple or too trendy – except possibly in its use of text messages. The image chosen shows young people, things that young people find interesting, or in the case of the picture of Dom Jolly, that the target audience finds amusing. **(6 marks)**

b) The layout and presentation of the leaflet is well suited to its young target audience. The main text is presented in short, easily read bursts of information each of which is clearly labelled with a sub-heading. The main heading and the 'did you know?' boxes are presented in an informal hand-written style that might have been produced by a young person in the first place. The illustrations break up the text and are of things like mobile phones' well-known comedians and attractive young people. **(4 marks)**

c) The newspaper article's main attention grabber is its headline, 'What's your poison?' This is quite a striking phrase but it is also familiar because it is sometimes used when people are offering a choice of food or drink. It turns out that the article is actually about poison but the reader has to investigate the article a little further to find this out. The second technique that the article uses is the sub-heading. This explains what the article is about but is also designed to increase reader curiosity as it contains a question. The language of the sub-heading is quite informal, using words like 'nasty' rather than, say, 'dangerous' or 'environmentally challenging'. The body of the article continues in an informal tone. It uses words like 'trash' and 'bin' and it even imagines a conversation 'What! You haven't got a digital widescreen TV yet? Loser!' The article seems to assume that people might be put off if a serious subject was taken too seriously. **(3 marks)**

GCSE model answers – PAPER 2

1 a) People love conkers. Or people hate clamper vans. Or we like to do ourselves down. Or we are plucky when we want to be. **(3 marks)**

b) John Lennon, or the Suffragettes or the man who invented the bobble hat are from the UK. **(3 marks)**

c) The advertisement begins with statements about 'UK' type opinions. These are almost inevitably stereotypes as the advertisers want to make a general statement about people in the UK that will not offend people. The conkers idea is meant to remind people of their happy childhood and the clamper van comment relates to shared adult annoyances. The statement about sports is a familiar one to explain UK teams' lack of success in games like soccer, cricket and rugby. The comments on doing ourselves down and pluck are meant to remind people of attitudes in the Second World War. If the advertisers had not used stereotypes, people would start disagreeing with the statements and would not be inclined to identify with UKTV. **(3 marks)**

d) Some people have tried to define Britishness in terms of race. Norman Tebbit's 'cricket test' was based on the idea that people who have come to live in Britain should support England even when it was playing their 'home' country. John Major used images of the past and of relaxed summers to define Britishness. He hardly mentions towns or cities at all but he does say that people like to do the football pools and love dogs. David Blunkett did not say what was British but said that things like forced marriages and genital mutilation were definitely un-British. **(6 marks)**

2 a) The idea that the advertisers seem to be aiming for in the text is a combination of the familiar and the slightly odd or eccentric. This makes the choice of picture very appropriate, as it shows two little old ladies at the seaside in what for many people will be a familiar image. In the background, however, there is a very strange dinosaur. No explanation is given and so the two parts of the photograph produce the same combination of familiar and odd that we find in the text. **(4 marks)**

b) We can tell that this ad is for a brand because it is not for any specific product or even programme. The logos at the bottom all have the initials UK in them and so the ad is trying to define what the idea of UK means to most people. Presumably the advertisers are implying that if you watch enough UKTV channels you will get a mixture of familiar and slightly odd programmes. **(4 marks)**

c) The article itself uses many of the techniques of ordinary newspapers. The headline uses a question to grab the readers' attention and there are a number of sub-headings to catch the readers' eyes and draw them further into the article. The article begins with the important facts and then provides plenty of examples to broaden the discussion. The added value is contained in the boxes around the story and in the images used. The quotations from famous people are interesting in a gossipy kind of way and the picture of the cricket screen illustrates something that people might not understand from John Major's discussion of Britishness. The boxes and pictures are generally useful in widening the range of opinions expressed in the article and giving the whole thing more balance. **(4 marks)**

ACKNOWLEDGEMENTS

The author and publisher are grateful to the copyright holders for permission to use quoted materials and photographs.

Every effort has been made to trace the copyright holders and to obtain their permission for the use of copyright material. The author and publisher will gladly receive information enabling them to rectify any error or omission in subsequent editions.

'Animal Magic' by Julie Myerson, The Guardian, March 20th, 2002. Copyright © The Guardian, 2002. Reprinted with permission; Advert for 'Dan Abnett: Straight Silver'. Reprinted with the kind permission of Games Workshop Limited www.games-workshop.com; 'I've Made Out a Will' and 'Mother, any distance' by Simon Armitage, from Book of Matches published by Faber and Faber, 1993, Reprinted by permission of Faber and Faber Limited.; 'Blessing' by Imtiaz Dharkar, from Postcards to God published by Bloodaxe Books, 1997. Reprinted with permission of Bloodaxe Books.; Short extract from Nineteen Eighty-Four by George Orwell (Copyright © George Orwell, 1949) by permission A. M. Heath & Co. Ltd, on behalf of Bill Hamilton as the Literary Editor of the Estate of the Late Sonia Brownell Orwell, and Secker & Warburg Limited.; Short extract from The Crow Road by Iain Banks published by Little Brown. Reprinted by permission of Time Warner Books UK.; Short extract from The War of the Worlds by H. G. Wells. Reprinted by permission of A. P. Watt Limited on behalf of Literary Executors of the Estate of H. G. Wells.; Short extract from A Room With A View by E. M. Forster. Reprinted by permission of the Provost and Scholars of King's College, Cambridge and The Society of Authors as the Literary Representatives of the E. M. Forster Estate.; Short extract from 'Your Shoes' by Michele Roberts, from During Mother's Absence published by Virago, 1994. Reprinted by permission of Time Warner Books UK.; Short extract from Growing Up by Joyce Cary. Reprinted by permission of The Andrew Lownie Literary Agency on behalf of the JLA Cary Estate.; Text and photographs from an Oxfam Leaflet 'bRing bring your old mobile phone to Oxfam'. Reprinted with permission of Oxfam GB, 274 Banbury Road, Oxford OX2 7DZ www.oxfam.org.uk.; 'What's your poison' by Oliver Bennett, The Guardian, October 19th, 2002. Copyright © Oliver Bennet, 2002. Reprinted with permission.; UKTV advert, reprinted by permission of Karmarama, London.; 'What is Britishness anyway?' from http://news.bbc.co.uk/1/hi/uk/1701843.stm. Reprinted with permission of the BBC.

First published 2006

British Library Cataloguing in Publication Data. A CIP record of this book is available from the British Library.

ISBN: 1843156636 (9781843156635)

Letts Educational Limited is a division of Granada Learning Limited, part of Granada plc.

Book concept and development: Helen Jacobs, Letts Publishing Director
Letts editorial team: Marion Davies and Tessa Fincham
Author: Frank Fitzsimmons

Cover design: Angela English
Inside concept design: Starfish Design
Text design, layout and editorial: Ken Vail Graphic Design

Printed and bound in Italy

ISBN 1-84315-663-6

9 781843 156635